# ZONES
### and CANADA

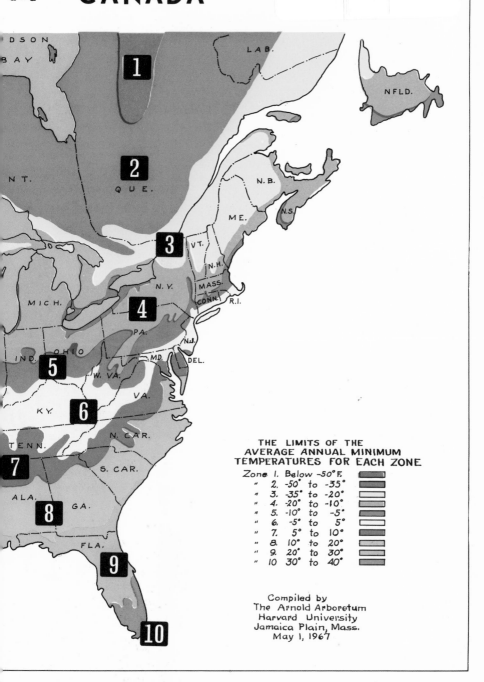

THE LIMITS OF THE
AVERAGE ANNUAL MINIMUM
TEMPERATURES FOR EACH ZONE

| Zone | | | |
|---|---|---|---|
| 1. | Below | −50° F. | |
| 2. | −50° | to | −35° |
| 3. | −35° | to | −20° |
| 4. | −20° | to | −10° |
| 5. | −10° | to | −5° |
| 6. | −5° | to | 5° |
| 7. | 5° | to | 10° |
| 8. | 10° | to | 20° |
| 9. | 20° | to | 30° |
| 10. | 30° | to | 40° |

Compiled by
The Arnold Arboretum
Harvard University
Jamaica Plain, Mass.
May 1, 1967

# Winterize Your Yard
# and Garden

# WINTERIZE
# YOUR YARD
# AND GARDEN

## by GEORGE TALOUMIS

*Photographs by the Author*

J. B. LIPPINCOTT COMPANY
*Philadelphia and New York*

*U. S. Library of Congress Cataloging in Publication Data*

Taloumis, George.
  Winterize your yard and garden.

  1. Gardening.  2. Lawns.  3. Plants—Winter protection.
  I. Title.
                SB454.T24      635'.04'9110973
                  ISBN 0-397-01178-4
Library of Congress Catalog Card Number 76–18862

In loving memory
of
Arno Henry Nehrling
Eminent horticulturist, outstanding
flower show director, compassionate
human being

# Contents

## PART 3 — Getting Ready for Spring

## PART 4 — Schedule for the South

# Foreword

THERE was a time—not too long ago—when the word "winterize" was practically unheard of, even nonexistant. It first came into use in connection with houses, then in relation to automobiles. Finally, the word crept into use with gardens, so that we "winterize" our gardens as well as our houses and cars.

My 1938 copy of Webster's Collegiate Dictionary, Fifth Edition, does not contain the word "winterize." My Webster's New World Dictionary, Second College Edition, 1970, does, and defines it: "to put into condition for or equip for winter (to *winterize* an automobile with antifreeze)."

As a boy I recall driving with my parents on winter Sundays to the wealthy oceanside suburbs of Marblehead Neck, Swampscott, and Nahant, just north of Boston, where evergreens and other shrubs were protected from strong winds and salt spray on the oceanside with boards painted green. Several years later wrapping with burlap came into the picture, not only at seaside estates, but in suburbs. Shrubs, chiefly evergreens, were covered with burlap and tied with string, often an ugly sight if not done carefully with attractive appearance in mind—winterizing the garden can and ought to be good looking. Nevertheless, it did the job—prevented shrubs from breaking from the weight of snow and ice, thus creating damage that was often irreparable or took years to rectify, as with aged boxwoods.

I remember from boyhood a pair of handsome arborvitae that graced the entranceway of a lovely old house that had a garden in front. In a severe snowstorm one tree snapped one third up from the base; the other did not. So they remain to this day, the one tall, towering, elegant, aristocratic, the other squat, rounded, compact, and stiff. With a single stake—or even tying with rope starting from the base and working upward—perhaps this damage could have been avoided.

Now we know it is best to take no chances. Besides, winterizing the garden has become a sophisticated art—if attractiveness is kept in mind, as it should be. Just about every home gardener practices it in one way or another. In addition to bracing trees, covering shrubs with frames and laths, hilling or placing collars around tender roses, applying mulches and winter blankets, using dormant and other sprays in late winter or early spring, relying on anti-desiccant sprays to cut down on windburning of needle and foliage evergreens, winterizing means cleaning up in the fall, planting hardy bulbs, lifting and dividing perennials, pruning from fall through early spring, setting out trees and shrubs, and tidying up after snow has melted or spring has finally arrived.

Today we have a great many aids to make a secure, healthy garden in winter possible, as well as easy. It is all a matter of knowing what to do and when, this depending largely on weather, and perhaps the first requisite for success is to get to know your climate as much as you can.

Many northern gardeners wrongly feel there is no winter in the South, at least not in the Deep South. They believe winterizing the garden is not necessary. For them the South is a warm, sunny land of swaying palms, oleanders and Chinese hibiscus, juicy oranges and grapefruits, and annuals that flower all winter long. While largely true, frosts do occur, so shielding and protecting plants in various ways is essential. Even in the warmest zones, 9 and 10 (see Zonal Map end papers), frost and ice will coat palms and other tropical plants, and tops of many will freeze to the ground, if not to the roots.

A friend, Frank C. A. McCulla, who for over twenty years has been editor of the *Bulletin* of the Men's Garden Club of Houston, Texas (zone 9), wrote me in a letter dated January 12, 1976: "Wish you would stop sending down that cold weather. It was seventy-eight degrees ten days ago, and a blue norther blew in and the temperature dropped to eighteen for two days. Everything in the garden froze. Today it is seventy-five and spring again."

So practically no matter where you live in the country—except in limited, minute areas (zone 10)—take some precaution, with certain tender plants at least, if you want your garden to come through the winter as unscathed as possible. The purpose of this book is to help you achieve that goal.

*Winterize Your Yard and Garden* is divided into four parts. The first three deal with the North. Part I covers what to do in gardens in the fall, Part II handles wintertime chores, Part III is concerned with spring care. Managing gardens in the short but vital winters of the vast Southland is treated in Part 4.

Many people helped to make this book possible. First and foremost I wish to express gratitude to my editor, Marjorie Goldstein, Special Projects Editor of The Literary Guild of America, who with ability, promptness, patience, and infectious buoyancy has seen me through this long ordeal. To Ruth Buchan, former editor of The American Garden Guild Book Club, who presented and inspired me with the brilliant and refreshing idea for this opus—"never done before"—and offered to wait a full year until I had time and was ready to embark on this undertaking. To Daniel J. Foley for sound counsel in this and previous books and for scrutinizing carefully Part 4 on the South. To Mrs. Arno H. Nehrling, who likewise went over this segment of the book. To Robert Fitzgerald, Regional Nursery and Floriculture Agent, Cooperative Extension Service, Essex Agricultural and Technical Institute, Hathorne, Massachusetts, for valuable up-to-date information and checking the chapter on "Pest and Weed Control," always keeping in mind the awareness and urgency to protect and preserve our natural environment. To the Arnold Arboretum of Harvard University of Jamaica Plain, Massachusetts, for the generous loan of their useful zonal map, encompassing the "Hardiness Zones of the United States and Canada."

Appreciation extends to the following gardeners and institutions in the North and South that willingly permitted me to photograph examples of protecting and caring for plants, features, and ornaments in their gardens from late fall through early spring: Mr. and Mrs. Moses Alpers, Kenneth Barry, Mr. and Mrs. Robert B. M. Barton, *Down East* magazine, Camden, Maine; Oliver Drackman, Essex Institute, Salem, Massachusetts; Daniel J. Foley, Heritage Plantation, Sandwich, Massachusetts; Hermann-Grima House, New Orleans, Louisiana; Mrs. Calvin Hosmer, Beverly James and Margaret O'Malley, Longue Vue Gardens, New Orleans, Louisiana; Nichols House Museum, Boston, Massachusetts; Mr. and Mrs. Louis Perles, Mr. and Mrs. Frank G. Ruggles, Harmon Saville, Mrs. Helen Taloumis, and Mrs. H. O. Wendt.

George Taloumis

*Peabody, Massachusetts*
*April, 1976*

# Part One

FALL CHORES

# 1

## What to Do with Leaves

WHEN THE FIRST LEAVES start to float down from tree tops—not those that drop in late summer from sickly trees, but from normal, healthy specimens—this is the signal that fall has begun, and it is time to winterize your garden.

Contrary to opinion, shorter days and cool weather—not necessarily a frost—will cause leaves to turn color. Their time just naturally comes, and it varies with the part of the country. Sometimes fall comes early, promoted by long droughts. Trees with ailments—elms affected by Dutch elm disease, maples by leaf scorch, lindens by Japanese beetles, and horse chestnuts by leaf blotch—will also shed sooner.

Gardens with several trees, shade and flowering, have great quantities of leaves to contend with—on lawns and in shrub and flower borders. Some leaves are needed as mulch, winter blankets, and the compost pile, but usually there are so many that some have to be disposed of—raked, shredded, or hauled away—or they will smother the grass and kill it.

There are several ways to get rid of leaves. The old tried-and-true method is the hand rake, still commonly used even in large gardens. It is, in fact, a familiar sight in the country where owners of old, large houses still rake the maple and oak leaves by hand. Hand raking is easy and actually a pleasurable task.

Rakes fall into two categories; garden and lawn. The garden rake, with its strong metal teeth, 1¾ to 3½" long, is not the one to use. Its purpose is to work seed beds after spading and to remove tufts of grass and stones, though there is a small four-toothed hand rake that is excellent for removing leaves that fall among shrubs. Used on lawns, these metal rakes pull up patches of turf.

The best kind is the ordinary bamboo or metal, commonly used to rake leaves. With cupped teeth that spring, it can be dragged over the ground to remove leaves without injuring the grass or digging into the soil. Occasionally a small patch or two of grass may loosen, more so in wet spots

*A bamboo rake with cupped teeth is one method to gather fallen leaves from lawns in the fall. The metal type is even superior since it springs back. Neither one will drag or uproot grass. If it happens, tamp with the feet.*

where turf is thin, and when this happens press it back into position with your feet. You can also use the lawn rake. It has sharp metal blades that will easily remove patches of crab grass and other weeds and loosen bare areas for reseeding. Or it can be used to prepare the soil for making a new lawn.

The matter of eliminating leaves from difficult spots like along fences, around clumps of small trees, among shrubs and late-flowering perennials (such as chrysanthemums, fall asters, Japanese anemones), and herbs (like lavender and santolina) is more tedious. A small metal or bamboo rake is recommended—a smaller version of the larger lawn rake. There are some impossible spots, however, in which you will have to kneel or gather leaves with your hands and dump them into a basket or box.

Where hand raking is not practical there are several kinds of mechanical machines that will do a better job and even pulverize leaves to apply as mulches or place in compost piles. One of these is the lawn sweeper, which by means of a stiff, rotary brush tosses leaves and other bits of debris into a large receptacle. Newer models cut broader swaths and have large containers. These sweepers, which vacuum leaves, are best for flat or gently sloping surfaces. They also come equipped with a hose attachment that works in tight spots and corners.

Leaf blowers are popular and are best on large lawns or on uneven ground where there are obstructions. By means of strong air jets, they pile leaves, twigs, and other debris into spots where you want them. Then they can be placed in large plastic bags, barrels, or old sheets and blankets, with the drawn corners tied for carting away, but be sure to step on the leaves first to reduce their volume.

Next is disposal, whether you haul them to the local dump or the municipality picks them up, which they often do to use as fill. Shredders cut leaves into small pieces, and some have chutes that toss them forcefully after they have been pulverized. A good shredder can reduce the volume of leaves up to 90 per cent, this including twigs, tops of annuals and perennials, and stems as large as corn stalks. The result is a fine mulch for the lawn or flowers, including trees, shrubs, and bulbs. The contents can be shot into a compost bin to be used for that purpose.

Rotary mowers come with or without bags. Those without bags will break up leaves partially, then gather them into piles. Those with leaf bags have good blades and a lifting motion that picks up leaves, shredding them partially as they are shoved into the bag. It is best to go over the area twice, remembering that large leaves from maple and plane trees crumble better than small leaves from birches and beeches.

Whatever method you use to get rid of leaves—and there are other kinds of machines that do just about anything you want—remember to save as many as possible and put them to good use. Small leaves like those just mentioned, along with willows, locusts, and crab apples, make good mulches because they curl and are light, allowing air to reach the roots. They make superb winter blankets, to be applied after the ground freezes hard. Avoid large leaves—maples particularly—as they flatten when wet and tend to smother and kill plants. Damage is worse if the cover is thick.

The one exception is oak, deserving of every praise. Though large, oak leaves curl and do not mat, allowing air to pass, thus preventing rotting. Use them freely around azaleas, camellias, hollies, mountain laurels, pieris, rhododendrons, and other acid-loving plants, because oak leaves have an acid content. Chrysanthemums, shallow-rooted perennials, often winterkill because roots are shoved upward by alternate freezing and thawing of the soil. To protect, either mulch or do not cut stems so oak leaves may fall and stay among them.

*Above, a mechanical blower puts quantities of leaves in neat piles, easier for discarding in plastic bags or barrels.*

*Below, a large shredder is recommended for substantial properties, though smaller models are available.*

*Leaves, as maple, elm, and viburnum shown above, can be used as winter mulch to protect bulbs and perennials.*

*Pull up annuals, as petunias, after tops have been killed by hard frost. If clean and non-diseased, use in compost pile.*

Be a conservationist by making a compost pile with entire or pulverized leaves and the dried tops of annuals, perennials, vegetables, and other plants. Among the latter, use only those that are disease and pest free. Dump them into a heap, mixing with dry manures or chemical fertilizers, as one pound of a 10-10-10 formula for ten pounds of dry leaves. Twice that amount of manure is needed. Mix in ground limestone to help speed up the decay process and lessen acidity. Leave a depression at the top to hold rain or hose water and support the sides with chicken or silo wire. In addition, apply compost activators, according to directions to help hasten decomposition.

When making a compost pile, the smaller the particles, the better. They decay faster, and you get quicker decomposition by turning over the pile often, as this aerates it and helps encourage bacterial action. Bacteria make for better root and top growth when the compost is spread on the vegetable—or flower—garden in the early spring. Weeds can be utilized for compost but take them before they have gone to seed.

Low fall and early winter temperatures deter decomposition speed. Get around this by placing a large piece of clear plastic over the compost pile, as the sunlight that passes through generates heat in the organic matter. Avoid black plastic because it obliterates the sun's rays, causing the plastic to become too hot, while the space between the plastic and the material beneath acts as a barrier, cutting off heat.

Making compost the old-fashioned way requires hard work and months for the completion of the fine, crumbly product. Devices and machines that hasten the process and cut down on the effort are available. Rather than a chore, making compost becomes a pleasure. And equally important, the compost pile—usually unsightly and generally placed where it is hidden from view—is attractive.

From England and available in this country comes an accelerating compost bin that converts grass, leaves, prunings, litter, and other organic matter into rich compost ready to spread in the garden in a few weeks. Materials can be added weekly, and since the bin is round—without corners—decomposition is quick. Air vents at the sides allow enough air to enter without loss of heat or moisture. Side panels slide up separately or collectively, enabling the gardener to shovel out the finished product from the bottom. Durable and non-rotting, a cover keeps the rain out, the heat in, and unpleasant odors that attract insects are eliminated.

Also available is a new piece of equipment that produces fluffy compost in just fourteen days, the only requirement being that once the material has been placed inside, it must be turned once daily for sixty seconds. This is done through a horizontal rotating drum, which at the same time protects the compost from the weather and retains needed heat. It is capable of holding more than fourteen bushels of material and is provided with screens at the sides and bottom for air to enter—necessary for the promotion of bacterial action. The drum, which turns easily, mixes the contents and hastens decomposition. The material can be loaded and unloaded into a wheelbarrow or other receptacle by a large removable door at the side. Water is needed only if dry material is used. New matter should not be added to contents in a state of decomposition, as it only stretches the time until the final product will be available for the garden.

Leaves can also be dug into the garden soil where they will decompose considerably by spring. Though they contain small amounts of nitrogen, they improve the structure of the soil and allow plant roots to penetrate more deeply, thus reducing the need of watering in summer.

Dry leaves grind more easily and finely, so use shredders, rotary, and other pulverizers when leaves are not wet. Remember that one obnoxious feature of many of these machines is that they make a raucous noise, so use them with discretion—during the middle of the day if possible.

If you remember one thing about leaves, it is this: do not burn. They are an asset no matter how used. Leaf burning also increases the amount of air pollution. Fortunately, most communities do not permit it. None should.

*Power mower with a bag will cut lawn for the last time in fall, and at the same time will shred and gather leaves.*

# 2

## Fall Lawn Care

TAKE A GOOD LOOK at your lawn in the fall. Is it healthy or does it demand special care? Does it require renovating, as most do, or will you need to start a new lawn from scratch? Without a doubt, fall is the best time of the growing season to take lawn inventory and determine what you should do to make it your pride and joy.

If your lawn is a bit shabby through neglect, drought, or a disease like brown patch, you can rejuvenate it if enough good permanent grass remains. Patches of weeds can be raked or pulled by hand, dug with a spading fork, and bare areas filled with sod, the best and easiest practice for late fall. It is also possible to sow seed, but this should be done earlier in the North, starting in mid-August, as it requires time to grow and become established before cold weather. An entirely new lawn can be made by seeding, but not late in the season in the North. Instead, wait for early spring. In the fall, sodding—a method that is simpler, quicker, more effective, and less expensive in the long run—is highly recommended.

To use sod, lift out straggly patches of grass and weeds and fill the area with new soil, scratching in mixed fertilizer. Then place the new sod carefully, tamping with the feet and making it level with the surrounding ground. It can be cut with a knife and placed in oddly sized patches where necessary. Water well and keep moist if the autumn is dry. With cool weather the sod will become root-established, and will soon fill in around the edges, giving your lawn a fresh, new look again. More details on use of sod are found in Part 3, Chapter 9 on "Important Lawn Care."

Should you prefer to use seed, scratch the area with an iron rake, turn over with a spading fork or shovel, level it, and pack. Distribute fertilizer with weed killer, digging in before broadcasting seed. Press and cover the fertilizer lightly with well-screened topsoil or pieces of burlap, to be removed later as seed begins to germinate. Water and keep the area moist. Generally, during sunny weather if the days are dry, allow the

*Use a lawn edger to trim grass along walks, terraces, flower borders, and other areas as late in fall as it continues to grow. Gather cuttings if thick and heavy.*

sprinkler to run twenty minutes in the morning and twenty minutes in the evening.

The advantages of fall sowing, if done early or in areas where the fall season is longer, are many. One is that warm days and cool evenings promote strong growth, especially if accompanied by rain. Second, annual weeds are at a minimum. If they appear, leave them alone as they will die in winter. Annual weeds grow more vigorously under the bright sun and longer days of spring. Forget about crab grass, as the season's crop will die out and in spring, when it germinates, you can apply crab-grass killers. Broad-leaved weeds, like dandelions, plantain, clover, and chickweed, can be killed with 2,4-D in the fall or spring on established lawns, following directions for use.

If sowing a new lawn—in the fall or spring—remember that peat moss is an excellent humus to enrich soil, hold moisture, improve aeration, and prevent nutrients from leaching through the soil. It is also sterile and free of weed seeds. If using lime or fertilizer when making a new lawn, fall or spring, use a spreader for even distribution. Before proceeding, think seriously about installing an underground sprinkling system, a great aid that will make lawn maintenance much easier, as one turf requirement is plenty of moisture.

The choice of turf, whether sod or from seed, depends on the part of the country in which you live. Before embarking on any kind of a planting program consult nurserymen and experts at state agricultural experiment stations. Kentucky and other bluegrasses are the first choice for lawns over a large part of the country—the North—where winters are cold and there is snow. Also recommended are fescues and bent grasses.

The trouble with bluegrasses is that they are subject to leaf-spot diseases from late May to late August. Though there is no such thing as a perfect grass, they are the closest embodiment—vigorous, disease free, able to withstand both heat and cold.

Doubtless the best of the bluegrasses is a strain known as Merion, the one recommended for the North. It also possesses high resistance to dreaded leaf-spot diseases, which are disfiguring to lawns.

There are several bluegrass strains worth considering, and perhaps you can locate the one best adapted to your climate. These include: Delta, Park, Arboretum, and Troy, all improvements, though susceptible to leaf spot. Windsor is moderately resistant to leaf spot, and Newport, with dark green blades, wards off powdery mildew and rust quite well.

The second lawn fall requirement, after seeding, is feeding. Recommended is feeding in the early spring and again in the fall, and this can be done late in the season even after leaves fall. Some experts advise an early summer feeding as well, but often it promotes a too-lush growth that is susceptible to brown patch and other diseases. Certainly spring and fall fertilizing suffice.

Normal feeding applications for lawns in the fall are ten pounds of 10-6-4, a high-nitrogen food, per thousand square feet. If using a 5-10-10 composition, apply twenty pounds for the same amount of area. Water well after feeding, to work the fertilizer down into the soil. A weed killer combined with a fertilizer can be substituted if weeds are a problem, but use amounts given on packages, no more, no less.

Highly practical are urea-form nitrogen lawn fertilizers, which are applied once a season either in the fall or spring. Spread at either time they continue to feed grass roots for the entire growing season.

Established lawns are benefited by fall feeding as grass continues to make new roots. If well fed, they are better able to resist leaf-spot diseases in the spring. Healthy lawns are also better able to ward off a disease known as snow mold, a common ailment that shows up in spring, if food is applied early enough so that strong roots and healthy blades develop.

Thatch—a layer of grass clippings, matted roots, and other dead plant material found at the base of the roots on ground level—should be removed in the fall. Dig it by hand or use a rake with flexible steel tines, though power tools are also available. If bare spots result, fill with sod or sow seed if early enough in the fall.

Next comes the matter of mowing, an important one not to be overlooked. It can be summed up briefly: continue to cut as long as grass grows, and this can vary widely from season to season. During the fall,

*Use a fertilizer spreader, above, to feed lawns in fall, when grass roots continue to grow even after cold days.*

*Hand mowers are still used by many gardeners, mostly on small lawns. Long, uncut grass will smother roots.*

set the mower to cut blades of grass shorter, as you do in the late spring. Left too long, grass will bend over, causing smothering and eventual killing of the roots. Ice that forms over grass and remains several days or weeks in midwinter will cause it to die, often as a result of snow mold. Packed hard, the turf receives little air.

If the soil of your lawn tends to be clayey and, therefore, hard-packed, aerate it before it goes into winter. On small lawns this can be done easily with a spading fork, digging the tines at regular intervals and working the fork back and forth, leaving holes through which air can penetrate. On large stretches this is tedious, and special machines that will do the job quickly with less effort are available.

*Lawn areas killed by brown patch disease in fall can be aerated with a rake. Grass may come back. If not, the soil can be removed and new added for sowing grass seed.*

# 3

## Setting Out Hardy Bulbs

ONE IMPORTANT GARDEN TASK must be done in the fall and at no other time of the year. It is the planting of hardy bulbs, usually known as Dutch. Original species of these bulbs, native to the Mediterranean and the Near East, were developed by the Dutch into the glorious hybrids we know today—mainly hyacinths, daffodils, and tulips.

Can you envision a garden, no matter how tiny, without a few Dutch bulbs? They have become an integral part of the horticultural picture, and with every good reason, for more than almost any other spring flower they announce that spring has come to stay, be it with the humble snowdrop or crocus.

What are the differences among bulbs, corms, rhizomes, and others given technical names? Though some flowers, as amaryllis, daffodils, and tulips, are truly bulbs, the word "bulb" is used generally and loosely for all kinds of bulbous plants—swollen underground stems. A corm, as gladiolus and ixia, is a solid, thickened stem base. A rhizome, as canna, is an elongated thickened stem. Dahlias have swollen, tuberous roots, while tubers, as caladiums and tuberous begonias, have thickened terminal portions of stems.

You cannot plant hardy Dutch bulbs in the spring and expect them to flower that season any more than you can pot them, set the container on a sunny window sill indoors, and anticipate blooms. These bulbs must go through a cool rooting period—not necessarily below freezing, but they need to undergo what is known as maturation, a chemical process that enables them to develop their flower buds. You can plant bulbs, as tulips, from a pot in the garden in the spring, but they must go through the cold of winter before blooming again.

Hardy bulbs can be planted as soon as they become available at garden centers or when the first leaves begin to fall. First plant the small bulbs—the miniatures, the winter aconites, the snowdrops, the crocus (for many the first sign of spring when they bloom), the scillas. Because they flower earlier—and sometimes this can be in mild weather in Janu-

*Fall is the time to plant hyacinths and other Dutch bulbs. A bulb planter, shown here, is handy to use.*

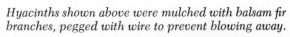

*Hyacinths shown above were mulched with balsam fir branches, pegged with wire to prevent blowing away.*

*Pink, blue, and white hyacinths around crab apple
in bloom the following spring. Later pansies were
set out, then wax begonias that bloomed all fall.*

ary and February in the cold North—they need a head start to develop
strong root systems.

Proper soil is important, with emphasis on good drainage, as bulbs
tend to rot if waterlogged. A light mellow soil is best, and whether sandy
or clayey, it can be augmented with peat moss, leafmold, compost, or
other organic material, which improve texture and provide needed nutrients. Turn the soil over well and mix in some bone meal or balanced fertilizer. Very heavy soils can be improved with sand or any of the inert
substitutes, as perlite, vermiculite, or terra-lite.

In certain places, as under high-branching trees or large shrubs, small
bulbs (like scillas and puschkinias) will naturalize; that is, spread and
seed themselves. So they require no care, except for an annual sprinkling
of mixed fertilizer applied in the late fall, early spring before flowering,
or after blooming has passed. Try naturalizing them under an early-
flowering tree or shrub, such as February daphne, Chinese or other
witch-hazels, Cornelian-cherry, or shadbushes. The bulbs will receive the
sunshine before the foliage develops and then go to sleep until fall, when
they start to make new roots again.

Daffodils and hyacinths, including hybrids, are also excellent for naturalizing. If you have a meadow or a plot of grass you do not need to
mow until late June or early July, you can naturalize daffodils. You can-

not cut the grass until early summer or until the foliage turns yellow and brown, so nourishment will go back into the bulbs for the development of next year's blossoms.

Though snowdrop, or galanthus (the Greek meaning milk flower), has the reputation of being the first to flower, actually winter aconite, or eranthis, comes before. It is a winter bloomer, as its name indicates, in warmer parts of the country. A member of the buttercup family, winter aconite produces gay, bright, yellow cups on three- to four-inch stems. Set them in well-drained soil three inches deep in sun—a rule that applies to just about all the miniatures. Spacing should be three to four inches apart in clumps of several bulbs for a more striking effect. Winter aconite is also ideal for rock gardens.

The more familiar snowdrop has white, bell-like flowers touched with green. Set it along the foundation of the house or at a spot visible from the kitchen or living room window, to be enjoyed in inclement weather. It too can be naturalized. If snowdrops bloom early in mild spells, they will just curl up, as if to keep warm, when it turns cold, then will thaw out when the weather warms again.

Ask anyone to name the first flower of spring, and he will doubtless indicate crocus, as he will name the robin as the first bird to arrive north in spring. Certainly both mean winter is no more. Yellow crocus often are first to bloom, followed by larger mauve, purple, blue, and white. Early varieties, Canarybird and E. A. Bowles, yellow; Mammoth Yellow; Enchantress, blue with violet base; and Snowstorm, are excellent Dutch hybrids. Planting depth of two to three inches and similar spacing is just right. As with all bulbs, do not remove foilage after flowering, but allow to ripen, when it pulls up with a gentle tug.

Many small bulbs are blue flowering, among them scilla or Siberian squill, a brave immigrant from Siberia that will multiply quickly under a yellow forsythia or soft pink saucer magnolia. Grape-hyacinth is a deeper blue (there is a white), and its spiked flowers resemble a small bunch of grapes. Heavenly Blue is a larger-blooming hybrid, and all muscari, to use the botanical name, make ideal companions for white, yellow, or orange daffodils. Chionodoxa, or glory-of-the-snow, is another wonderfully small bulb that flowers a little later. It is a member of the lily family. Starry flowers appear on upright stems, and pink and white varieties are available.

White flowering are summer snowdrops or snowflakes, also called leucojums, with exquisite tinkling bells at the tips of foot-tall stems with slender leaves resembling daffodils. Two fritillarias, common in Dutch flower paintings, are the checkered lily or guinea-hen flower (*Fritillaria meleagris*) and crown imperial (*F. imperalis*). The first grows a foot tall, with hanging checkered purple or maroon flowers about three inches across (there is a white form). The other is tall and regal, three or four feet high, with orange-red or yellow flowers on stems with whorled leaves. Shooting up quickly in the spring, it makes a startling display not easily forgotten when first seen. Crown imperial requires a very well-drained soil, with some lime added. Be certain to allow foliage to ripen after the memorable display is over. These bulbs do not like to be disturbed once happily established.

The big three among Dutch bulbs are daffodils, hyacinths, and tulips; all very colorful. Hyacinths, sweetly fragrant, are excellent for bedding. They are formal in nature, to be placed around a sundial, birdbath, lamppost, mailbox, or small tree. Light, sandy, well-drained soil is a must. Plant them five to six inches deep, six to eight inches apart, usually in October in the North; true of daffodils and tulips as well. Colors are many, and some well-known varieties include: King of the Blues; City of Haarlem, creamy-yellow; La Victoire, rosy-carmine; and the old-time favorite L'Innonence, white.

Jaunty daffodils or narcissus, a name applied to all kinds, are show-offs. They flower just after or at the same time as hyacinths, and are ideal to plant around forsythias, as both bloom simultaneously, an effective combination. If you want to naturalize daffodils, simply scatter by the handful, and plant where they fall, but try to keep several of the same variety together, avoiding mixtures.

Daffodils can be planted even in November in the cold North, when leaves have completely fallen from trees, but strive for October planting so bulbs will develop strong root systems, Spacing depends on the size of the bulbs, as well as desired effects. Large bulbs need six to eight inches; small four to six. Set large bulbs five to six inches deep, and smaller four to five.

Some good varieties include: King Alfred, a large yellow; Mount Hood, white; and Spellbinder, greenish yellow. There are double-flowered kinds, as Mary Copeland, creamy-white-yellow; and poeticus or poet's daffodils, as Actaea, white-yellow-crimson. Medium trumpet types include Aranjuez, yellow and orange. Two other classifications are the dainty jonquils and miniatures, as Yellow Petticoat, the best known.

Tulips are stately and lend themselves admirably to formal plantings. In home gardens, they are ideal along both sides of a front walk. Like hyacinths and daffodils, tulips can be planted any time in October and into November where temperatures go below zero, providing the soil is workable. Do not wait too long, as an early start usually gives better results.

Plant about six inches deep with the pointed ends up. If placed at a depth of eight to ten inches, bulbs do not have to be lifted and separated as often. With shallower setting, dividing is advised every three or four years. Mix some bone meal or superphosphate, slow-acting fertilizers, into the soil. This is recommended for all hardy bulbs.

Types and classifications are too many to mention. They include: Darwin, as Orange Sun; Cottage, as Golden Harvest; Parrot, with frilly petals, as Blue Parrot; and the rose-pink-green Fantasy. The white Mt. Tacoma is a double peony type. Lily-flowered is represented by the yellow West Point, and Fringed by the lilac-blue Blue Heron. Also available are species and botanical tulips. Two of the best known are Red Emperor, a Fosteriana hybrid, and Kaufmanniana, a white-and-yellow species.

Finally come hybrid lilies, truly the most queenly and largest flowering hardy bulbs. Of all hardy bulbs, they can be planted latest, as long as the soil is soft and workable, because they come into flower in summer and fall, rather than in spring. Lilies demand exceptionally well-drained soil, well provided with organic matter; sun for at least part of the day, and a sheltered location. They are tall growing, large blooming, and easily flop over unless staked.

Hybrid lilies flower at varying times. You can enjoy continuous bloom from June until frost. Enchantment is a popular mid-century hybrid. Madonna, which requires shallow planting (two inches deep), blooms in June and makes a fine companion for delphiniums. Regal is white, flushed with yellow, sweetly fragrant. Speciosums may be pink, crimson-red, or white. Perhaps the most splendid of all are the Auratums, in several colors. The season ends in September and October with the white Lilium formosanum. Small varieties can be set five to six inches deep; larger need nine to fifteen inches. Mulching after planting is advised.

# 4

## How to Handle Tender Bulbs

ONE OF THE MOST important fall chores, both before and after frost, is that of lifting and storing tender bulbs for the winter. Tender means bulbs that cannot remain in the ground all winter or they will die.

What is and what is not tender varies, of course, with the region of the country. Generally, hardy bulbs can withstand temperatures well below freezing and the zero mark without any protection whatsoever. Tender, including basket-flower or ismene, calla-lilies, cannas, dahlias, gladiolus, montbretias, tigridias, and tuberous begonias, cannot. Yet some of them —dahlias and gladiolus chiefly—are considerably tough and able to survive winters in the ground where temperatures go well below freezing. Usually they are in protected areas close to the house, where they receive "heat" from the basement, and gardeners who have discovered that they do not have to go to all the effort of lifting and storing them apply a thick mulch, insuring their survival even more.

These summer-flowering bulbs, as they are also called, bloom over a longer period of time than the spring bulbs, providing much color for the summer and autumn garden.

Although there are slight variations in treatment, bulbs are stored by the same basic method. Generally, after waiting for a light frost to blacken the leaves, lift the bulbs carefully with a spading fork and allow them to dry in the sun or in the open air for several hours. Cut off the leaves if browned or blackened, and store the bulbs in containers filled with a medium like peat moss, sand, perlite, vermiculite, or soil. Put them in the basement or other cool place—such as a closet—where winter temperatures will not go below freezing. Nowadays plastic bags, tied closely, are much used—with or without a medium—and are excellent because they hold in moisture so bulbs do not dry out. At the same time, they allow enough air to penetrate for the bulbs to breathe and not rot.

An anti-desiccant spray, as Wilt-Pruf NCF, can be applied to tender bulbs before storing to help them keep better. Bulbs may also be dipped in a solution of four parts water and one of Wilt-Pruf NCF just after dig-

Dig dahlia tubers after tops have been blackened by
hard frost. When using a spading fork, keep a safe
distance from the bulbs in order not to injure them.

Allow the tops and bulbs to dry in the sun or open air
for several hours. With sharp shears, cut off about
four to six inches from the base of the bulbs.

*Store dried tubers in pans or cartons as they are, in perlite (shown here), vermiculite, peat moss, or sand. Garden soil is also an excellent medium.*

ging. When dry store in boxes in any of the mediums mentioned above.

From this general routine, some bulbs vary in the way they are stored. With experience and through reading books and articles you will learn the requirements of each bulb. Dahlias, for instance, increase abundantly, so your stock will be greater each year. Dividing time is not until spring, but then you will have more for yourself and plenty to give to friends or for garden sales. With others, like tuberous begonias, the same bulb keeps increasing in size, which means larger plants and more blooms. The same bulbs, as with the tender gloxinias, usually grown as pot plants in the North, will live ten years or more. Yet they can be cut into sections with a sharp knife so you can increase your supply. Each section, however, must have an eye or visible bud or swelling that will develop into a sprout—a simple matter as several eyes are generally produced.

With dahlias, after lifting when tops have blackened, do not knock the soil off the tubers but allow some to cling as it helps to retain moisture

*Some bulbs, as basket flower or Peruvian daffodil, are tender so tops get limp with a slight frost. Lift carefully so roots, needed for the blooms, are not cut.*

and keep out air. After drying outdoors or in the garage for several hours, cut the stems back to three or four inches, place in bushel baskets, cartons, or plastic bags, and cover with peat moss, sand, perlite, sawdust, or other medium. From experience I have found garden soil to be excellent, particularly for today's warm basements, which compared to old-time cellars are warmer and drier. Tubers can also be placed in thick layers of newspapers or burlap.

Another aid is to dust stems and bulbs with sulphur as this helps to prevent rotting caused by disease organisms present in the soil and, therefore, on the bulbs. Bulbs need a temperature of forty to fifty degrees, but fare well at warmer readings if soil is used as the insulating medium.

Gladiolus are simple to store, largely because you do not have to wait for a frost to bring them in. Leaves start to yellow and brown—that is, cure—after flowering is over, usually four to six weeks after the spikes have faded. At that time simply lift the corms, allowing soil to cling and taking care that the stems do not break off (the continuing ripening process of the leaves is needed for better flowering). Spread out the corms for two or three days if the weather is not rainy, or place them in the garage or basement.

You will find that the original corm has shriveled and dried, but that others have been produced at the sides. This is normal. It is best to remove the original before storing, but it can be left until spring when the clumps are separated for planting. Spraying with Sevin will help to control thrips (a common pest) and then, after cutting off the dried leaves, store in open boxes, trays, and other containers, or in plastic bags. A storage medium is not needed but keep as cool as possible—the same as dahlias.

As with dahlias, wait until frosts have killed the large leaves of cannas. The strong deep roots are more difficult to lift, and two persons, each with a spading fork, may be needed for some specimens. After lifted, cut stalks back to six inches with a sharp pruning shears, shake off excess soil, and store in the same manner as dahlias in a cool place. In the spring cut large clumps into smaller sections, each with one or more eyes or buds that will grow into sprouts, and for earlier bloom in the garden give an early start indoors, planting in trays or large pots in March or April at the latest.

The lovely tuberous begonias, which grow best along the west coast and the northern shores of New England, succumb earlier because of their tender, succulent leaves and stems. Lift after a slight frost has blighted the leaves. Place plants as they are, with the tops attached, in trays, flats, or shallow cartons in a dry place, as a basement, for tops to brown completely. This may take a week or more, and when it does, tops break off easily. Then shake off the soil, dust with sulphur or ferbam to thwart diseases, and store in boxes, cartons, or plastic bags in peat moss, sand, or other medium at forty-five to sixty degrees.

Peruvian daffodil (or ismene or basket-flower [*Hymenocallis cala-thina*]) should be dug when the straplike leaves, similar to those of amaryllis, have softened with the first frost, as they will because they are succulent. Work the spading fork carefully around each bulb in order not to break the roots. Without removing the leaves, allow to dry in a warm place, fifty-five degrees or above, a temperature they will need all winter. Lower readings will kill next year's flower bud already present in each bulb.

The lesser-grown montbretias and colorful tigridias that brightened your garden in summer can be handled in the same way as gladiolus. Dig the corms after frost, easy to do because they are small. Without dividing, place in a dry airy place for a week before storing in the usual manner.

Caladiums have been becoming increasingly popular because of their gay, exotic, papery leaves and their ability—and preference—to thrive in shade where splashes of color are often needed. Dig bulbs after touched by frost, which will be early as their thin leaves are very delicate. Dry in the sun or open air, without cutting the foliage, and take to the basement or shed where leaves are allowed to turn completely brown. Then store in peat moss, sand, or perlite in boxes or plastic bags in a place that is warm, 60 to 65° F., nothing less than 50° F. Like tuberous begonias, bulbs increase in size every year.

Nowadays, calla-lilies—the traditional white and yellow with white-spotted leaves, and the smaller pink—are being grown in the open ground more and more. They withstand considerable cold, and in sheltered areas of the Northwest, will survive outdoors. Treat them like gladiolus, keeping at forty-five to sixty degrees for the winter.

If you've grown fragrant tuberoses for the first time, you might have been disappointed to learn that you cannot store bulbs for a second flowering. The usual policy is to throw them away after blooming and start with new stock next spring. You can try to store them at sixty degrees or higher and separate the bulbs in the spring just before planting them. When setting outdoors place in a hot spot as they are heat lovers, and even when started outdoors, they are inclined to flower in September and October in the North.

There are other tender, summer-flowering bulbs—tenderness, of course, depending on where you live. It's fun to experiment with new kinds, as the lovely trailing achimenes, much grown in window boxes and hanging containers in the warm, humid South; the gloriosa or climbing lily; summer hyacinth (*Galtonia candicans*), with creamy-white, bell-shaped flowers, a native of Africa; and Dutch and Spanish iris, actually quite hardy, able to survive cold winters in the ground, but added to this group because they are summer flowering and far too little grown.

# 5

## Lifting and Dividing Perennials

PART OF CLEANING up the garden and getting it ready for the winter involves the lifting and dividing of large, weakened, overgrown clumps of hardy perennials. It is best to start just about the time the first leaves begin to fall as this gives plants time to develop strong root systems and become well-established before cold, freezing weather.

Hardy perennials fall into three groupings: early bloomers, midsummer bloomers, and late-flowering plants. The early bloomers include: arabis, bleeding hearts, blue phlox, gold-dust, cerastium, crested iris, ground phlox, iberis, polemonium, primroses, violas, violets, and Virginia bluebells.

Midsummer hardy perennials include: ajuga, anchusa, astilbe, balloonflower, baptisia, bee-balm, blue flax, cimicifuga, columbine, coral-bells, coreopsis, daylilies, delphiniums, doronicum, gaillardias, gasplant, geum, globe-thistle, hostas, hybrid physostegias, iris, Japanese and Siberian iris, lupines, lythrums, monkshoods, Oriental poppies, phlox, pinks, shasta daisies, and thermopsis.

Late bloomers, which should not be disturbed until spring because they are still flowering late into fall—in an active state and not dormant —include aster Frikarti, bocconia, Christmas rose, chrysanthemums, fall asters, heleniums, helianthus, heliopsis, hibiscus or rosemallow, leadwort (*Ceratostigma*), mistflower (*Eupatorium*), monkshood, perennial phlox, and the many stonecrops (*Sedium spectabile*), among them the deeply hued varieties like Autumn Joy and Meteor.

Fall is the best time to lift and divide the early and midsummer bloomers for several reasons. First, soil is warm and soft, and there are apt to be autumn rains. Days may be warm, but not evenings. In spring soil is inclined to be too cold and wet to work, and it often rains— frequently on weekends, the only time many of us have to garden seriously. Most of all, perennials lifted, separated, and planted in the fall are ready to start their spring growth without interruption and setback,

When hardy chrysanthemums have faded, cut tops to
ground, leaving stems four to six inches high. Stems
can be cut up in a mechanical shredder for compost.

Marsh hay, light and airy, is an excellent material to
protect chrysanthemums for the winter. Another way is
to leave stems uncut to catch leaves that fall from trees.

very important with early bloomers which do not perform well if disrupted in spring. This is also true of flowers that bloom in midsummer —in June, July, and August.

Whether you will lift and divide dormant perennials now, as you should or in the early spring, because of necessity, the procedure is basically the same. Lift plants carefully with a spading fork or shovel, separate into divisions, and retain the outer shoots, which are usually younger and more vigorous. Prepare the soil with organic matter and slow-acting fertilizer, water, and mulch. Proper soil preparation is the most important consideration since most perennials, including fast spreaders, stay in the same spots about three or four years.

Small, shallow-rooted perennials, as ground phlox and lamb's ears, lift easily with a spade, a small spading fork, or a shovel if necessary. Larger types will definitely require the standard spading fork or a large shovel. Very large specimens—kinds that can remain in the same spot for many years, as hostas and peonies—may well require the strength of two men, each with a spading fork, working around on all sides, loosening soil, until plants come up. Some may even need an ax or a large sharp knife. Peonies and rosemallows are outstanding examples.

Spreading perennials (ajuga, bearded iris, bee-balm, chrysanthemums, fall asters, and perennial canterbury bells) fall into one category—plants whose strong, outer shoots should be retained. In these perennials the centers tend to be weak, often dead and woody, best thrown away. The outer category includes plants that are strong and healthy throughout, so that all divisions may be kept for replanting. In this grouping fall amsonia, baptisia, cimicifuga, daylily, gasplant, hosta, liatris, Oriental poppy, peony, and rosemallow. These are the kinds that are best left undisturbed, in the same spot, for many years.

The first step after lifting is proper soil preparation. Dig deeply with a spading fork, whether the location is the same or new, turning the earth to a depth of twelve to eighteen inches. Next spread and dig in some organic matter to enrich it, make it more friable, better able to retain moisture. Use peat moss, leafmold, dehydrated manures (old, rotted if you can get it), compost, shredded bark, or wood chips.

If the area has been fed yearly, fertilizing will not be necessary, but slow-acting foods, as dry manures, compost, bone meal, and superphosphate, can be mixed into the soil. Roots will benefit from this application when they will grow as the soil—and weather—stay warm. In spring they will profit more and proceed into active, undisrupted growth and flowering. Do not use quick-acting chemical fertilizers as they can spur late-season growth that may cause winterkilling if the weather continues warm into November and December.

Except in small and narrow areas, put groups of three, five, or more plant divisions together, depending on space and the desired effect next

*Large clumps of hostas can be lifted and divided in the fall. Use a spading fork, working it in slowly all around so that the roots will come up easily.*

*Hosta after lifted, showing the large size of the clump. Hostas are very hardy so they can be separated late in the fall, but do not wait too long.*

Very large clumps of hostas and other perennials may require two spading forks to separate them into sections. Use one fork for the rest.

Hosta after divided in thirds. Before planting, cut off leaves if they have started to yellow. Hostas do well in shade, even if quite dense.

In the fall, lift and separate large, sparsely flowering clumps of bearded iris when they are dormant. Outer fans, younger and more vigorous, are ones to keep.

With iris toss out weak or dead inner portions. Before planting outer shoots, cut fans back to about six inches. Borer infested rhizomes should be discarded or burned.

*Plant iris in groups, keeping to one variety, setting close to the surface. Rhizomes require covering with an inch or two of soil. Apply some humus, then water.*

season. Smaller kinds can be six to eight inches apart; about a foot for larger. Spacing also depends on how often you divide. Some perennials, like chrysanthemums, fall asters, lamb's ears, and sedums, perform best if lifted and separated annually.

Set the plant divisions so their tops are level with the surface of the soil, fill in with soil, and tamp with your hands, feet, or a shovel if necessary. The purpose of pressing the soil is to eliminate air. Always leave a depression at the top to hold rain or water, and be certain to soak plants well especially if soil is dry. If it does not rain, water every three or four days. With very hardy kinds, as daylilies, hostas, and phlox, mulching is not necessary, but in general is advisable. Use a light, airy material—marsh hay, straw, evergreen branches—after the ground freezes hard and before snow flies.

*To tidy up the garden, cut dead tops of hardy peren-
nials back to ground with sharp pruning shears. Shown
here is amsonia, a handsome blue-flowering wild flower.*

Special caution is needed for peonies. If planted too deeply, they will
not flower no matter how many years pass—ten, twenty, or more. To get
blooms the following season, allow each division at least three or four
visible red eyes or buds that will develop into shoots in the spring. Set
with the eyes or buds about an inch and a half below the surface of the
soil, no deeper. More peonies fail to flower because of too-deep planting
than because of poor soil, lack of feeding, or insufficient sun.

In addition to attention paid perennials, seeds of several hardy annuals
can be sown after leaves fall from trees. They germinate early in the
spring and gain a head start. The list includes very hardy kinds, and
these vary with the section of the country. Some of the hardiest include:
annual phlox, bachelor's-buttons, calendula, California and Shirley poppies, cleome, flowering tobacco, larkspur, snapdragons, and sweet alyssum.

# 6

## Winter Care of Roses

THE ROSE, no matter where, still remains the Queen of Flowers. It is so today as it was in ancient times when the Grecian island of Rhodes was named after this lovely flower which grew in abundance on it.

Today the rose is so highly bred that it tends to winterkill unless protected in the North or to be short-lived in the warmer South, where it does not have a long enough dormant period. Wherever grown, it needs some kind of special care, never regretted because it is such a beautiful flower.

Gardeners in the North, where temperatures often go well below freezing and the zero point, are beset with the greatest problems. For instance, tender roses will survive winter better if plants are not fed after midsummer. Gardeners should avoid a high-nitrogen fertilizer which promotes soft, late growth. This growth does not have enough time to harden sufficiently before cold weather. Well-nurtured plants, not fed late, often come through the winter without protection in cold parts of the country.

With hybrid teas and other tender roses in your area, protect your plants with the idea that the winter will be a severe one—take no chances. The first step when it comes to growing roses is to find which are considered hardy where you live and which are not. For instance, the Father Hugo rose and other species, as well as hardy climbers like Paul's Scarlet and New Dawn, are stronger in general and need less protection. There are variations within a state, even in a matter of a few miles, especially along coastal regions, and local government experiment stations can be of help. If there is a local unit of the American Rose Society nearby, consider joining it.

The old-time method for wintering hybrid tea and other bush-type roses, which still works well today, is hilling with soil taken from another part of the garden and not around plants, so you don't expose roots. I know one rosarian who has been growing roses in the greater Boston area for over thirty years and still swears by this method and no other.

*A tried and true method of protecting roses where cold
is to hill with soil to height of about eight inches.*

Plants should be hilled with soil to a height of eight to twelve inches just
before the soil freezes hard.

After that, when the soil solidifies, plants should be covered with a
thick blanket of marsh hay, straw, evergreen branches, or other light,
airy material that does not mat or smother. Several barriers can be used
to prevent the soil from washing away, like chicken wire or small baskets
with bottoms removed. Easier and more attractive are the dark green
plastic rose collars that are circled around each plant and fitted with
tabs. If plants are close together, the collars can be made smaller and secured with staples. They are about seven inches high and after put in position are filled with soil, which does not wash away in the heaviest rains.
They can be stored and used over and over again.

A more recent collar is a mesh type, like green window screening, with
the advantage that drainage is excellent and there is no danger of wa-
terlogging. Made of fiber glass, they are called Fiberglas Rose-bush Winterizers and will not rot, rust, or mildew. Each is simply placed over a
plant after branches are tied together, and the centers filled with soil.
Peat moss is also an excellent medium because it is light and porous, permitting water to drain and allowing air to reach the stems and roots
when weather is warm and the peat moss is not frozen. Compared with
rose collars, rose winterizers are less conspicuous, though neither is offen-
sive. After removing in the spring, they can be washed, rolled compactly,
and stored for reuse.

*Formal beds of hybrid tea roses can be protected with soil, straw, and burlap that can be stored for reuse.*

Some old-time rosarians who still believe in soil mounding cover their plants with bushel baskets, and better still a taller, tapering kind, narrower at the bottom than the top, used by farmers to package and sell vegetables. They are durable and long lasting and can be reused for several years. It's all a matter of what you prefer and what experience has proven works best for you. The important point to keep in mind is that roses in colder climates do require some form of winter protection.

Still more recent are the Styrofoam cones or hoods that guarantee roses warmth and safe dormancy. To anchor the larger size (about twenty inches high) against the wind, place a heavy rock on top. Smaller hoods for shorter plants, ten to twelve inches, can be held in position with soil packed around the base or with bent pieces of wire coat hangers.

The drawback of Styrofoam cones is that they act like a greenhouse in early spring, promoting premature growth with the first warm weather. You will need to provide ventilation by tipping them a little, and when days are warm, the cones can be removed for the day. If plants are well hardened, tops can be taken off in mid-March in the North with little or no damage.

For climbing hybrid teas, the usual method is to loosen canes from their supports, bend them over carefully until tops touch the ground, and

Wooden frames to protect roses are sturdy, long-lasting, and attractive, particularly when painted a dark green. Styrofoam cones for protecting roses are relatively new. Place stone on top to prevent wind from blowing them over.

*If using rose-bush winterizers, which look like screening and are made of fiberglass, first tie stems with string. Position the rose-bush winterizers over every plant, then fill with soil taken from another part of garden.*

then cover with a thick layer of marsh hay, straw, litter, evergreen branches, or other material, so nothing blows away. Wooden structures with straw or marsh hay inside are recommended for plants in extremely exposed places, as along the seashore, in treeless newly developed areas, and in the open Great Plains.

Tree roses in cold climates are the most sensitive of all when it comes to winter damage, usually resulting in complete winterkilling. The old method—and still hard to beat—was to dig plants entirely, roots and all, and lay them in a trench, covering completely with soil. Easier is the technique of leaving plants in position, making a large hole at one side, and removing soil, bending stems so that they are parallel to the surface of the ground as much as possible. Cover the stems, tie the tops with soft string, then add soil and leaves or other litter. So much and so successfully practiced is it in the cold state of Minnesota, where temperatures often plummet to 30° below zero, that it is known as the "Minnesota Tip Method." Needless to say, the heavy blanket of snow that comes there early and lasts all winter long acts as an insulation. The method is used for hybrid teas, floribundas, and other tender roses in the northern states.

Where it is less cold, stems of tree roses, along with lower branches, can be covered with strips of tree wrap, starting at the bottom and working upward spirally. Then cover with straw or marsh hay held in place with two or three thicknesses of burlap. There is also a tree rose winterizer you can buy, but it is expensive—astronomical if you have many plants. Plants remain as they are, in their upright positions, without any digging or disturbance, and are able to withstand temperatures to 18° below zero. The winterizer is a polyvinyl-chloride frame with aluminum folding arms and insulating foam sides which last many years.

Another method with tree roses is to cover stems and crowns with straw, hay, or marsh hay held in position with burlap. Each plant has a stake as it will not stand up on its own, but insert another to insure added security against cold and to hold the protective materials in place. This is not recommended for the coldest areas of the country but works well where winters are not too severe, yet below freezing with snow and ice.

If you grow tree roses in tubs, large pots, or other containers, they can be wintered safely in their containers in a cool basement, cellar room, or shed where the temperature does not go below twenty degrees. In late winter or very early spring, before growth starts, bring them to the garage, where it is cooler, and keep the doors open when weather permits. On mild days containers can be taken outdoors so they will adjust without premature growth, then taken into the garage for the night if weather gets too cold. This works well, but it does require facilities, labor, and time.

Container-grown roses can be set out in the fall, the sooner the better where very cold. Prepare the soil well.

Rest the container rose in the hole so that the top of the ball of soil is an inch below the level of the ground.

*Roses can be protected with rose collars, solid plastic and green, filled to the top with a shovelful or two of soil.*

*Pruning a climbing rose in the fall. Be certain to tie well with Twist-ems, and as with all roses, go light on pruning.*

*It is essential to secure climbing roses to their supports, whether on fence, trellis, or arbor. Canes can be fastened with Twist-ems to nails or hooks, looped rather loosely.*

What about pruning? In one word: none. You can cut away weakened dead wood and shorten long canes that will beat about in the wind, but the winter itself will result in a certain amount of inevitable winterkilling. Let nature prune first. Cuts made in the fall are not apt to heal, particularly if growth is soft.

Other precautionary measures should be taken. Secure climbers to their supports, particularly new canes, using Twist-ems or soft string that does not bruise or cut into the stems. Also, remove leaves around plants as spores of black spot disease can attack them during winter. This is more essential near the seashore or in moist sections of the country.

Lastly, apply a mulch or winter blanket after the ground freezes hard, which might be early November or early December, depending on where you live. It is the best insulator, guaranteed to keep the cold in the ground, the temperature even, and prevent fluctuations of thawing and heaving that occur when days change from cold to warm and vice versa. It's the covering that will keep roses—and other plants where used— warm.

# 7

## Planting Trees and Shrubs

LATE FALL and early winter are among the best times of the year to plant new trees and shrubs. Done then, it's another chore out of the way leaving more time for the rush of spring. It is important that the tree or shrub be planted with proper care. Unless set out correctly, it may die, often not immediately and forcing you to wait a year or two to make replacements.

The first step in proper planting is to determine the right location. Do you want a shade or flowering tree? Do you want the tree near the house for summer shade or as a lawn specimen? Large shade trees will need a distance of fifty feet between them while small trees can be anywhere from twelve to fifteen apart. With shrubs the same principle applies, so first learn the plant's ultimate size if you intend to let it grow with little pruning. A spacing of five to eight feet is normal; with smaller, three or four feet will suffice. With annual pruning twice a year, large and small shrubs can be kept as low as three or four feet for decades without shearing (not recommended except in well-designed formal gardens). Since the ground remains warm late in the fall and early winter, even after a crust forms on the surface of the soil, root formation continues. Thus, newly set out trees and shrubs become firmly established before soil freezes solidly and really cold weather sets in.

As a rule, keep to very hardy trees: American and European lindens; Norway, red, and other maples; oaks; and plane trees for deciduous. Crab apples, dogwoods, Oriental cherries, and shadbushes are excellent small flowering trees. For evergreens consider arborvitae, Colorado blue and Norway spruces, red and Scotch pines, and tall Japanese yews. Among shrubs select azaleas and hardy rhododendrons, including the early-flowering Korean azalea, beach plums, black alder, mock-oranges, privets, and shrub dogwoods and honeysuckles.

Leave those a bit tender or questionable for spring when warm weather follows and the danger of killing partially or completely by win-

*Brace fall-planted trees against winter winds. One depend-*
*able method is known as guying. Pass wire through pieces of*
*hose to protect bark. Attach to stakes at equal points in ground.*

ter cold is eliminated. When setting out plants considered tender in the
northern limit of their range (as American and English hollies, blue
hydrangea, cherry laurel, English ivy, and mahonia) where temperatures
often hover around zero, select, if possible, a northern exposure without
winter sun. Less damage is apt to occur when soil is frozen and leaves
are unable to replace moisture they lose. Injury from sun is known as
sunscald; that from wind is called windburning.

Once you have decided what and where to plant, the next step is soil
preparation. It is basic, of extreme importance, corresponding to a sturdy
foundation of a house. If you are going to do the job, do it well or don't
bother at all. Good drainage cannot be stressed enough, and if soil is
heavy, lighten with sand, peat moss, perlite, vermiculite, or compost. The
same treatment applies to light soils, which are improved by the addition
of organic matter or inert drainage materials.

If you have wet areas in your garden, remember that certain trees and shrubs grow well there. They are American arborvitae, aronias, azaleas, highbush and lowbush blueberries which turn orange-red in the fall, hollies, larches, mountain laurel, red maple, red osier and yellowtwig dogwood, rhododendrons, shadbushes, shrub dogwoods, spicebush, summersweet or clethra, sweet-gum, tupelo, viburnums, and willows.

Always make a hole larger than the ball of soil or the spread of the roots if dealing with bare-rooted specimens. Many trees and shrubs planted in the late fall after leaves have fallen are shipped through mail without the ball of soil because they are lighter. Evergreens are always handled with a ball of soil as they are always in leaf. The hole should be approximately one-third deeper and one-third wider than the spread of the root system.

When digging the hole, place the good topsoil to one side in a separate pile, keeping the poorer subsoil in another heap. After the hole has been dug toss a shovel or two of good topsoil at the bottom as it will come in direct contact with the roots. Then scatter a few handfuls of bone meal, superphosphate, dry manure, or compost, but not chemical fertilizers as they are too fast acting. The nutrients will go to work slowly, benefiting plants as they start growth in spring. On the whole, avoid too much food, particularly with bare-rooted specimens as root growth must come first. Once this occurs and plants are established, they can be fed again.

Whether it's a tree or shrub, set so the obvious soil line—the base of the trunk or the base of the branches, white below, dark above—is at the same level with the surrounding soil. In other words, rest it in the same position as it was in the nursery, or maybe an inch or two deeper, but no more as it can be harmful. This is a reason tree wells are constructed around trunks covered with fill during the building of new houses.

With bare-rooted stock, spread roots out in all directions, throw in some topsoil, step on it with your feet to eliminate air, and firm. Add more soil until about three fourths of the hole is filled. Then apply water with a soaker, or a hose with the nozzle removed, slowly so it soaks in thoroughly. After water has drained add more, and when it has leached through add the remaining topsoil and finally the poorer subsoil. Do not, however, use all the soil, in order to leave a depression at the top to catch rain or water applied from the hose. After this tamp firmly again with the feet and add a mulch.

With balled and burlapped specimens take care not to disturb the roots or allow the ball of soil to break apart. After placing the tree or shrub in position loosen the burlap after untying and tuck in around the base. Then add topsoil, pressing and tamping with the feet or a thick piece of wood, as a section of a tree trunk. Water, add more soil following the same procedure, and in time the burlap will decay to turn into valuable, nourishing organic matter for the roots.

*Evergeens, as hemlock, can be planted in fall. Make a large hole, enriching the soil with peat or other humus.*

*Rest ball of soil in hole. If covered with burlap, untie and tuck in. If plastic is used, slash with sharp knife.*

*After pressing-soil with feet, soak deeply. One way is
to remove nozzle from hose. Or use a soil soaker.*

Trees and shrubs often come with the ball of soil wrapped with plastic. This is an aid to nurserymen since plants do not dry out as quickly and require watering less often. As with burlap, untie, slash the plastic with a sharp knife for roots to penetrate or cut out large pieces with scissors, taking care that the ball does not break apart. Do not pull the plastic (it decomposes slowly compared to burlap) from under the ball of soil. Better not take the chance, as the knife-slashing method has proven to be successful. Remember to leave the depression at the top to hold water, and to add the mulch.

If you have planted a tree, it is advisable to cut some of the branches back so any roots destroyed in the digging and planting will have less top to support. Cut out some of the lower branches, V-shaped crotches, any branches that cross or rub against one another, and those that are dead or weak. If cuts are wider than an inch, cover with tree-wound paint, applied with an aerosol bomb or a can and brush to seal, keep out water, and prevent diseases from entering.

*With trees, cover barks with tree wrap to prevent winter injury known as sunscald. Use pieces of old hose to prevent wire from cutting into bark. Leave supports at least two years.*

Next, cover trunks with tree wrap or strips of burlap or raffia paper, wound spirally around, starting at the bottom. This is to prevent dehydration and sunscald resulting in bark splitting, which is caused by strong rays of the sun. Straw and marsh hay are other materials that can be substituted, wrapped in three- to four-inch layers around trunks and tied with rope or wire. Secure so material will not fall during the winter from the weight of snow or ice. Warm days with sudden drops in temperature cause the cracking of bark. Trees with thin barks, as birches, cherries, and magnolias, are more susceptible to this problem. The wrapping should be left on two to three years in very windy places. Though scar tissues may form over the splits, they may occur again the following winter.

*Before planting a tree or shrub, mix humus, as peat moss,
in hole then add a handful or two of mixed fertilizer.*

Recently available is a durable weather-resistant vinyl that twists easily around barks of young, newly planted trees. If necessary, it can be removed to examine bark, and then be replaced. Requiring no taping or
tying, it is ventilated, permitting air to reach the bark. In addition, it expands to accommodate new growth. The new vinyl comes in twenty-
four-inch lengths.

Fig and other trees not hardy in the northern limit of their growing
range can be wrapped entirely (usually they remain small in the North)
with burlap or heavy paper. Another method is to loosen roots at one
side (as practiced with tree roses), bend trunks over, and cover tops
with soil and litter. Where it is especially cold for figs (and other tender
trees or shrubs), dig plants, roots and all, and bury entirely in a trench.
Apply a thick mulch after the soil freezes hard.

Last and most important of all is staking. Without it many a newly
planted tree will lean or topple over. Those in extremely windy places, as
the seashore or the open plains, need it the most, although new trees in
cities, where drafts among high buildings can be strong and damaging,
need to be staked as well. Like tree wrap, supports should be kept at
least two years, better three, four or more in windiest locations.

Supports can be tall, strong wooden or metal stakes pounded into the
ground close to the tree trunk. Secure lowest branches with heavy wire
passed through sections of hose so you don't injure or cut into the bark.
Larger trees will need three or four stakes placed at equidistant points
around the tree, at an angle away from the trunk. Depending on the
location—chiefly the amount of wind—keep in place two or three years.

When the root ball is wrapped with burlap, as with this
kousa dogwood, first untie, then loosen, next tuck in
around the sides (where it will decay) before adding soil.

Final step is staking. This small kousa dogwood is easily
tied with several strands of rope to two wooden stakes.

# 8

## Tree and Shrub Care

TREES AND SHRUBS require special late fall care: feeding and pruning. Given this attention, established trees and shrubs sail through the winter smoothly, benefiting from feeding, as roots keep on growing after leaves fall, and pruning which cuts down on the amount of damage created by the elements—ice snapping and heavy snow breakage.

It is remarkable how well garden and street trees survive, growing year after year in alien environments where they are deprived of the leaves—through raking and sweeping—that nature supplies to replenish the soil. We rake leaves from lawns where, if left, they would nourish trees and shrubs; we leave trees surrounded by pavements that cut out natural food supply, unless they are fed, which they usually are not.

In gardens the situation is somewhat better, though it is surprising how many gardeners feed flowering plants and lawns yet leave trees and shrubs to fend for themselves, falsely thinking their roots dive deep into the soil where there is nourishment and moisture.

When trees are not fed and nourished they show it more than shrubs, which are smaller and require less moisture to begin with. Foliage in upper branches of trees becomes sparse, many branches die back, growth slows down, and in the case of evergreens, winds suck moisture from leaves during winter, causing them to turn brown in late spring or early summer.

Trees often lack sufficient amounts of nitrogen needed for healthy growth. An overall yellowish appearance may be caused by a low supply of iron. Stunted growth may mean insufficient amounts of phosphoric acid, which promotes strong root growth and the production of carbohydrates, stored for the following season's growth. Brown patches resembling scorching may be a potash lack, needed to strengthen and ripen wood.

Both November and early December after leaves have dropped are an excellent time to feed established trees and shrubs. Nourishment is absorbed into the trunks and branches, ready to be utilized with warm

*Removing V-shaped crotches from crab apple in fall.*
*A large portion of branch is cut first, then the stub.*

*Cuts are made flush with main trunk for appearance.*
*Tree paint is sprayed to keep out moisture and diseases.*

spring weather, stimulating vigorous growth. As long as the ground is not frozen, the food absorption process goes on. Even in January in the North, when there is a thaw, or in February, you can feed if you cannot get to it in the late fall. The sooner it is done the better, as trees and shrubs will be ready for their strong leaf and flower production. Plant food helps overcome weaknesses caused by summer dryness, insects or diseases, and excessive heat, which often scorches leaves, especially large ones like maples.

The only time to avoid feeding established—and newly planted—trees and shrubs is from mid-July until the end of September or October when leaves start to fall. This is because fertilizer might stimulate late abnormal growth that may be winterkilled. During this period spring and early summer growth should be hardening to withstand winter's cold.

The fine-feeding roots of trees and shrubs are not located close to the base, but at the outer tips of the branches or the so-called "drip line." Some of these roots extend beyond and within this circle, and some may stretch vast distances in search of moisture.

Homeowners can feed their own trees and shrubs with a crowbar and a highly organic food like 10-6-4. Make holes eight to twelve inches deep or deeper if the soil is soft, between one and a half and three feet apart, depending on the size of the tree or shrub. With small shrubs, the holes do not need to be as deep. A very large tree may need as many as a hundred holes, though fewer will suffice. In either case—tree or shrub— follow directions on the package for proportions of fertilizer to apply. Give that amount and no more.

With trees, the percentage of fertilizer depends on the diameter of the trunk. The average is five pounds per inch of trunk at a foot or two above the base. In order not to injure lawns where there are specimen trees, take circular sections, make holes, and fill with fertilizer up to three or four inches of the surface. Then replace the turf. Shrubs are more easily fed with a hand trowel. Or use a root feeder, which plunges deeply into the soil to distribute food to the feeding roots where needed. If turf is not removed, simply make holes with a crowbar or root feeder.

Although a high-nitrogen formula is recommended, indicated by a high first number, as the 10-6-4, sometimes a different combination, like 4-8-7, may be required. Obviously undernourished trees may need phosphorous or potash. A new and easy way to feed trees is with fertilizer spikes, which are hammered around trees at the feeding roots. If the ground is dry, water it, for all fertilizers are activated by moisture. Besides, it is essential that trees and shrubs go into the winter with their limbs and twigs turgid with moisture. Applying a mulch after feeding will help retain moisture in the soil.

Trees and shrubs can be pruned in the late fall. Shrubs are simpler than trees as they are more easily reached, and a steady stepladder will

Repairing a dogwood damaged by a tree that fell on it. Split branches were tied to others and sprayed with tree paint, and covered with tree wrap to aid healing.

To feed and strengthen the dogwood, holes a foot to a foot and a half deep were made with a crowbar all around, at the feeding roots at tips of the branches.

*To feed, a trowelful of mixed fertilizer was placed in each hole, then covered with soil. This was done in November, a good time to feed trees as roots still grow.*

*New lush growth the following summer on the side on which the large tree fell. Note upper branches still fastened with rope. Blooming in May was very profuse.*

*Where not reliably flower bud hardy, blue hydrangea needs winter covering. After tying branches with rope, wrap several layers of burlap around, tied to stakes.*

make it easy to reach the tops of the tallest. With trees you are limited. Small ones, of course, are easily pruned to a point where a ladder permits. This applies to large trees, in the case of removing lower branches, but beyond that it is hazardous. The average home gardener should not climb large trees to prune as it involves a liability not worth the risk. Engage tree experts, who are well-trained and climb high, cutting dead and superfluous branches with a pole pruner. They are fully insured so their company is responsible for any injuries. Good pruning is skilled work, worth every dollar you are willing to pay.

If you cannot both feed and prune in the late fall, then feed, leaving pruning for the winter when it can be done on mild days. Even in severest climates there are pleasant days as winter draws to an end when you can get out into the garden to prune—when it is a welcome change, and when you feel that spring is that much closer.

What to prune? With trees and shrubs the basic rule applies: remove dead, weak, and diseased wood. Then thin to let in more air and sun. In one way, pruning after foliage has fallen is easier because leaves do not get in the way. In another, more difficult since you cannot detect dead and weak wood as easily. Try, if possible, to make mental—or written— notes of tree branches you want to remove in the fall or winter. In windy places prune tops of trees more drastically to thin and allow strong winds to pass through with less obstruction. This is especially recommended for large, prized specimens, which topple when soil is soggy during periods of excessive rainfall.

Always remove V-shaped crotches, as they are weak and tend to split in storms, often straight down the middle of the trunk. Eliminate branches that rub against each other or crisscross. To control size, shorten outer branches at varying lengths to maintain the natural shape of each kind. Then open up to shape, adhering to the basic principles of design— proportion, scale, and balance. Be certain to cut dangerous limbs and large branches that hang over sidewalks and driveways, or over houses and garages. If they break in ice or other storms, they can cause much damage. Where V-shaped crotches on large trees are too high to reach, engage an arborist and he will do the job well, particularly for a large, handsome specimen or a historic tree on your own or community property. In the case of the latter, garden clubs often bear the cost of aged trees of historical or other significance.

Always work with well-sharpened tools, make cuts flush with the trunk or branches (never leave stubs), and cover cuts an inch or more in diameter with tree-wound paint, which acts as an insulator.

Fall pruning is basically light pruning, mostly to avoid winter breakage and lighten the load of spring work. Very hardy trees and shrubs can be pruned hard, just as you wish, without injury. However, there are certain tender trees and shrubs—ones that suffer considerable dieback even in mild winters—that should be left for the spring. What these are depends on your area, as hardiness is a relative term. In the North, with much below freezing and under zero weather, this includes Atlas cedar, Chinese redbud, common paper mulberry, cryptomeria, English holly and oak, as well as yew, flowering dogwood (it gets bud-killed), hardy form of cedar of Lebanon, hardy orange (*Poncirus trifoliata*), Judas tree (native to Europe), Oriental plane tree, silk tree, and western hemlock.

Among shrubs, allow winter to "prune" the following which fall into the tender classification in the North: blue hydrangea, butterfly bush, caryopteris, cherry laurel, Chinese snowball, English boxwood, fig (*Ficus carica*), harlequin glorybower, holly osmanthus, Japanese holly, leatherleaf mahonia, rosemary, scarlet firethorn, strawberry bush (*Euonymus americana*), vitexes, and wax-myrtle.

# 9

## Pay Attention to Hedges

Too LITTLE THOUGHT is given the winter protection of hedges, yet they do need special attention, particularly formally clipped evergreen types like yew and boxwood. Once broken by snow or children they often take more than a season to recover—sometimes three or more.

The appeal of neatly clipped formal hedges, straight or undulating at the tops of sides, rests in their preciseness, their geometry. Many are those, including non-gardeners, who admire formal hedges that are so well cared for they seem unreal. This does not apply so much to informal hedges, that is those allowed to grow naturally, as forsythia or vanhoutte spirea, pruned just enough to remove dead and weak wood and to control their size. They recover more quickly if smashed, and the gouges are not so evident.

Though it is wise to brace informal hedges with fencing or stakes with wire stretched across the sides, we are dealing here more with formal evergreen and deciduous hedges. More stress should be placed on those in formal gardens, often edged with low boxwood, Ilex crenata microphylla, or gray santolina. Sometimes individual plants are broken so badly they require replacement, but they still take a year or two to fill in. Evergreens take more time than deciduous as they are generally slower growing, a reason they cost more than deciduous trees and shrubs initially.

A formal evergreen hedge can be a tree, like Canadian or Carolina hemlocks, both common; holly oak (*Quercus ilex*), hardy in the southernmost parts of the country; Sawara false cypress; and Austrian and white pines. The selection of shrubs is greater, and most formal hedges, evergreen or deciduous, are shrubs up to five or six feet, rather than trees. Among evergreens they include arborvitae; American and English hollies, though they become large trees; convex-leaved Japanese holly (*Ilex crenata convexa*); Hick's, Hatfield, and Japanese yews; and winterberry barberry (*Berberis julianae*).

Deciduous trees include American beech; European hornbeam, common in the formal gardens of Europe; littleleaf linden; and shingle oak

Kingsville boxwood hedge along a walk protected from windburning and snow breakage by covering with branches of balsam fir.
Evergreen branches, green all winter, make an attractive covering.

Below, the same hedge in summer after new growth had developed, showing how plants came through unscathed though snow
was excessive. Old Christmas trees can be used for this protection.

*Formal yew hedge protected with boards from ocean salt spray, as well as salt from sand dumped on road behind. Stakes are needed to brace boards where winds are strong.*

(*Quercus imbricaria*). Without the least doubt, deciduous privets in the North, like Amur and common, are the most versatile, inexpensive, quick to grow, drought resistant, and excellent kinds to depend on. They are followed by Japanese barberry, a rather ratty shrub that somehow never looks neat and tidy, and the superior upright Mentor and red-leaved forms of barberries. In the warmer South, evergreen Japanese privet takes the place of deciduous kinds in northern gardens. It has larger leaves, up to four inches long.

Other good deciduous shrubs for hedges include five-leaf aralia (*Acanthopanax sieboldianus*), common lilac, dwarf Arctic willow, forsythia, hypericums and potentillas, small shrubs with yellow flowers in summer and fall; Japanese flowering quince, better grown informally than formally; mock-oranges, and shrubby dogwoods and honeysuckles. With flowering hedges such as Chinese hibiscus, glossy abelia, lilac, and mock-orange you must bear in mind that much bloom is sacrificed in shearing.

*Hedges along driveways especially need protection. This privet is guarded by strong wooden posts and rope along the sides, making it safe from shoveling as well as blowers.*

The first method for safeguarding hedges against the winter elements is to spray evergreen types with an anti-desiccant material, like Wilt-Pruf NCF. By coating leaves, yet permitting them to breathe, windburning is eliminated. When the ground is frozen solidly, the sun is shining and the wind is blowing, leaves give off moisture they are unable to replace. As a result they turn brown, though this does not show up until late spring or early summer. Follow directions carefully for use, and for best results give a second application in February or early March when temperatures are in the high forties. With the new Wilt-Pruf NCF two applications can be given ten days apart in the early winter.

The second method—and more important—involves mechanical props. This might be chicken wire for a low hedge, secured to metal or wooden stakes inserted at regular intervals. Stakes should not extend beyond the

*Wire fencing braced by metal stakes will guard hedge along a sidewalk from snow shoveling and children.*

*Below, same privet hedge on January 28 showing gaps made by children when it was not protected by a fence.*

*Pruning same privet hedge to remove broken branches.
Pruning and feeding stimulate vigorous growth.*

*Keep on clipping deciduous hedges, as privet, barberry,
and five-leaf aralia, as long as growth appears in fall.*

*Instead of hand shears, electric shears can be used when clipping deciduous hedges in fall. If possible avoid on boxwood because of "burning" (leaf browning).*

wire, as they would then be unsightly and more conspicuous. Insert larger stakes for taller hedges and secure strong wire across, best along both sides but at least on the sidewalk and street facade. Stakes and wires are less conspicuous and equally effective.

Snow fences will do the same thing and are the most attractive of all. They are recommended for driveways or sidewalks where snow blowers or snowplows dump large mounds of snow at great force directly on the hedge. Needless to say, they stand little chance of bearing up well, more so if the winter happens to be a very snowy one.

In large cities, as New York, Philadelphia, Chicago, and Boston, where apartment buildings have hedges along small plots at the front, custom-made wire or metal fences can be installed that stay put all year around. Painted black—perhaps dark green—branches of hedges will grow through the openings to conceal the framework entirely. They can be clipped along the sides and across the tops. A garden area need not be large to be attractive. It is not size but quality that counts, and in these small spaces such an investment is worthwhile. This fencing will also protect plants inside the hedge from snow, vandals, and dogs.

Another technique is to cover low hedges (dwarf and Korean box-woods, dwarf Japanese barberry [*Berberis thunbergi minor*], Ilex crenata helleri, lavender, pachistima, and santolina) with evergreen branches such as balsam fir or white or other pine. The boughs are green and alive and remain so in the cold northern winters. To be certain the wind does not blow the branches away, secure here and there with wire or string to each other or peg down with bamboo or other stakes. Evergreen branches applied in this manner help to prevent breakage from snow and ice and cover plants, guarding them against windburning.

Deciduous hedges can be sheared as long as they continue to grow, which can be well into October in the North. If they have not made appreciable growth by late fall when winter sets in, do at least cut off straggly shoots with pruning shears. Generally, evergreen hedges make early summer growth and then stop, except for an occasional wayward shoot which you should trim back before winter.

Informal deciduous hedges can be improved in appearance and kept young and vigorous by cutting some of the oldest branches directly to the ground. This will induce new shoots from the base. You can cut them back in the fall or early winter (that is, very hardy kinds) with no win-terkilling. For borderline kinds—a bit tender—wait until spring as winter will do much of the "pruning" for you.

Finally, if you cannot protect them from snow damage in advance, do at least get in the habit of shaking newly fallen snow from hedges, again paying more attention to evergreen types.

# 10

## The Vegetable Garden

THE MORE CARE the vegetable garden is given in the late fall, the better the next season's crop will be. If nothing more, old crops must be pulled up and discarded or put to use in one way or another, the soil must be turned over and lime applied. If you plant a cover crop, known as a green manure, you will get off to an even better start and insure a high yield next summer.

The first step in the vegetable garden involves cleaning up, digging up crops that have served their usefulness once killed by frost, such as beans, corn, eggplants, and tomatoes. Some vegetables, including beets, broccoli, Brussels sprouts, cabbage, carrots, celery, fennel, Jerusalem artichokes, and squash, are not harmed by early frosts. The flavor of kinds that grow in the ground is improved when plants are touched by frost, a better time to harvest them. In the early winter they can continue to be useful for several weeks. One vegetable that should be left in the ground until after hard frosts is turnip. Radishes and potatoes are others that are not prone to chilling, and onions should be pulled only after their leaves have flopped over.

When pulling vegetables like cantaloupes, corn stalks, cucumbers, beans, tomatoes, and watermelons, knock off the good garden soil around roots. Tops can be handled in various ways. One is to place them in barrels or plastic bags to be collected as rubbish—a waste. A second is to use them as organic matter, as humus, replenishing and improving the soil for next year's crops. Disease and pest-free tops, still partially green or browned by hard frosts, can be dug in rows in the ground. First dig a trench about a foot deep, spread the tops in the trench at a thickness of three to four inches and cover with soil. By spring the unwanted tops will have decayed.

There are some pulled-up plants that should not be used as organic matter because of the problems they can create. Tomatoes may carry over bacterial spot and canker diseases. Spent turnips and cabbages can result in black leg and black rot, and potato peels will leave a disease

*Disease-free corn stalks cut with clippers and placed on soil of vegetable garden for winter can be turned under as organic matter in spring. Cabbage and Swiss chard are at rear.*

known as verticillium in the soil to infect next season's crop. European corn borer will overwinter in stalks that are dug into the soil, even after cut into smaller sections, as is necessary. If you are unsure about the health of the vegetable tops, do not use them.

A preferred practice is to use these vegetable tops—even ones that may be diseased—for the compost pile. The stalks should be shred into small pieces so they will decompose rapidly. Interestingly, many disease organisms and pests are destroyed when pulverized by heat action created in the compost pile, and this includes the European corn borer. Details of making a compost pile can be found in Chapter 1 of this section.

To prepare the vegetable garden for the following spring, dig or plow the soil—by hand if the patch is small, or with a rototiller if large. This has many advantages, mostly that the soil is ready for spring planting.

*Soil in vegetable garden can be turned over with rototiller in fall to be ready for spring planting. If possible spread agricultural limestone so it will have time to dissolve.*

Tilling combined with winter freezing helps improve the soil structure by breaking apart the squeezed soil particles, while at the same time allowing water to penetrate more easily. When you spade, work in a layer of limestone, which aids in reducing acidity, a result of a loss or depletion of calcium. Limestone applied in the late fall has all winter to dissolve and is superior to quick-acting hydrated lime applied in the spring, which often burns in cases of overdosage.

The best fall preparatory measure is to plant a cover or "green manure," guaranteed to insure a better vegetable garden next spring. A cover crop does many things. First, it adds humus when the growth is turned under in the spring. Second, it supplies nitrogen, one of the most important needs in the vegetable garden. Third, it helps rains from causing soil erosion, and fourth, it reduces wind damage, especially where winters are dry and there is little or no snow coverage. Annual rye grass is considered the best and least expensive of green manures for home gardeners in the North, along with hardy winter rye. Annual rye grass will form lush growth when sown in September in the North. During the course of the winter it will die and decompose, adding humus and nutrients to the soil when spaded under in the early spring. Hardy winter rye is considered superior because it continues to develop its roots and tops in the

*Tops of disease-free vegetables can be pulverized through an electric grinder in fall for the compost pile.*

*For decomposing organic matter of all kinds, the compost bin is an essential item for every garden.*

*Everbearing varieties of raspberries can be pruned in fall, then mulched heavily with light and airy straw.*

*Braced dwarf apple tree, with wire screening around trunk to protect bark from mice and other animals.*

early spring, after its short growth in the fall. In spring, when eight or ten inches high, it should be cut with hedge shears then finely pulverized with a power mower before working into the soil with a spading fork or rototiller. Buckwheat and alfalfa are other excellent cover crops.

One important perennial vegetable that requires its own brand of winter attention is rhubarb. Using your hands, clean out the old, dead outer leaves but do not cut any that are green. Remove seed pods and then mulch lightly with straw, marsh hay, leaves, or other airy material around the base when soil freezes. Asparagus, another perennial vegetable, requires little care—simply cut tops to the base when they have turned brown.

What about fruits? With them the most urgent fall measure is sanitation, which helps prevent the spread of diseases and pests the following season. Rake leaves, which carry disease spores, and with them gather fruits that have dropped. Apply a mulch, but leave space around the trunk so mice will not nest there. On small fruit trees, encircle trunks with an eight-inch collar of one-quarter-inch mesh hardware cloth to prevent mice and other rodents from nibbling at the bark.

Small fruit bushes, as blackberries, blueberries, and raspberries, do not require much care. Allow leaves that drop to remain around the base, and when the ground freezes apply a light mulch. On fall-planted specimens—both fruit trees and brambles—apply a thick mulch. Gather leaves beneath established grapes, mulch when the soil freezes hard, and prune in the late winter or very early spring before sap begins to flow.

# 11

## Fall Care of Herbs

INTEREST IN HERBS has increased markedly in recent years as more and more people who love cooking discover their wonderful flavoring possibilities. Steeped in lore and tradition, herbs make attractive garden plants as well, if only for sprigs taken and rubbed between the fingers as one wanders in the garden.

Growth, given light well-drained soil and sun, is simple. Winter care of herbs boils down to the matter of knowing which are perennials and which are annuals and treating each accordingly.

Well-known and much-grown perennial herbs generally hardy even where winters go well below freezing include bee-balm, bergamot, chives, fennel, garlic, ginseng, horehound, horse-radish, lavender, lemon-balm, lovage, mints, sages, salad burnet, santolina, snakeroot, tarragon, teucrium, thymes, and winter savory.

Annuals for cold or warm climates include anise, borage, chervil, coriander, dill, parsley (a biennial), summer savory, sweet basil, sweet fennel (a perennial treated as an annual), and sweet marjoram.

With hardy perennials, tops should be cut down after blackened by frost. Degree of hardiness determines the need to cover or mulch. Where winters are severe, a light airy mulch, as marsh hay, straw, or evergreen branches, is advised to be applied after the ground freezes hard. The plants may also be protected with bushel baskets, boxes with openings, sheets of plastic, likewise with openings for air to pass through, or pieces or sheets of burlap. Oak or other leaves that do not mat when wet are excellent to place around them for protection.

Perennial herbs that are not hardy, and these include lemon verbena and rosemary in the North can be relegated to the cold-frame or potted and wintered in cool plant rooms, greenhouse, or breezeways. Small specimens of both perennials and annuals can be taken up in the fall and potted to grow in sunny windows—chiefly kitchen windows where they are more appropriate and can easily be snipped to flavor food.

*Perennial herbs, where tender, will need protecting for winter with a light mulch, which allows air to enter.*

*Protecting golden sage with marsh hay, one of the best mulches, which can be gathered and stored for reuse.*

*Costmary lifted from garden and potted in fall and grown all winter in a sunny kitchen window. Do the same with others, as parsley, mints, pineapple, sage, and chives.*

Use a sandy soil with a little low-nitrogen fertilizer or bone meal added. Herbs you can bring indoors include catnip, chives, costmary, lemon verbena, mints, rosemary, and sweet marjoram, as well as caraway and parsley, both biennials. In the spring these herbs can be planted in the garden or in containers—particularly earthenware pots where they look more natural and which provide excellent drainage, an important requiste for herbs of all kinds.

Very hardy perennials, among them bee-balm, bergamot, chives, costmary, mints, and tansy, can be lifted and divided in the fall in the North. Others of questionable hardiness or kinds that die back in the North (as lavender, santolina, teucrium, all subshrubs—often treated as edgings in rose gardens) are separated in the early spring. In the warmer South, fall is a safe time. Herbs that die back, like lavender or santolina, should be pruned in the spring after winter has done its damage. On healthy, established plants, new growth is lush and rapid.

Spreaders, as bee-balm, costmary, mints, and thymes, need annual separating to retain their vigor and to prevent them from encroaching on other nearby plants. This can be done in the fall or spring depending on hardiness in your area. If uncertain, it is always safe to wait until spring.

# 12

## The Importance of Winter Mulches

MOST GARDENERS KNOW about summer mulches, their purposes, and that they can be applied at any time of the growing season. Few know about *winter* mulches that are spread around plants in early winter at the time the ground freezes hard. Fewer still are aware of the winter *blanket,* a mulch, but thicker, applied at the same time and for the same purpose, but on plants that are more tender and less apt to survive winter's cold.

What is the difference between a winter mulch and a winter blanket? A winter mulch is simply a thin layer of peat moss, wood chips, marsh hay, shredded leaves or another material placed around plants to keep the temperature in the ground as even as possible, and thus thwart the ill effects of the alternating freezing and thawing of the soil, which sends roots upward causing damage or death to the plant. A blanket is usually a thicker layer of marsh hay or straw—or other material—around hybrid tea roses or oak leaves around perennials, to be removed in the early spring before vigorous growth commences. Shallow-rooted perennials like chrysanthemums need it most, along with lavender, lupines, and tritomas, which in colder regions are usually not hardy outdoors and must be wintered in a cold-frame. With these care must be taken regarding materials used as some will simply mat when wet and cause suffocating.

If our gardens were comprised of native plants totally—those that abound in each area—there would be no need for a mulch or winter blanket. The plants would be adapted to localities and able to fend for themselves as they have for centuries. But our gardens contain more exotics—that is, non-natives, not to mention hybrids—that are tender and delicate, as well as plants grown in the northern limit of their hardiness range.

Plants that keep green leaves all winter, known as rosettes, need mulches especially. Madonna lily and Oriental poppy are two outstanding examples. Three well-known biennials with green leaves all winter are canterbury bells, foxgloves, and sweet williams. For these plants the mulch must be light and airy, such as straw, marsh hay, or ev-

*Winter mulch of straw around rhododendron. In spring some can be left to decompose. Collect most of it, store in a basement in plastic bags or cartons for reuse in the fall.*

ergreen branches, and it must be placed under and around the leaves, lifting them up from the ground carefully to prevent rotting. Some mulch can be spread over the leaves, but not much, so sun and air can get through. It is enough if roots are protected.

You need to get the mulch in place before a heavy blanket of snow falls, which would then make the task impossible. Snow actually is nature's best winter blanket, but we cannot always rely on it. If early snow were to stay all winter, it would be ideal; but it does not. That is why gardeners in northern areas can grow plants which winterkill farther south where the climate is warmer. An open winter with little or no snow causes more damage than one with snow on the ground all winter. Most northern states do not have the assurance of snow that the northern continental states (away from the oceans), as Minnesota, Montana, and the Dakotas, do.

Mulching is also highly advised for plants newly set out in the fall. This applies to trees and shrubs, as well as perennials, herbs, and bulbs.

Straw placed around lilacs in fall, loosened in spring to let in air, but allowed to remain for the season as summer mulch.

Balsam fir branches—Christmas trees—placed on a bed of Dutch bulbs as winter blanket to be removed in early spring.

*Where wind in open spaces and large rodents like squirrels are a hazard to Dutch bulbs, use a frame with wire screening. A winter blanket placed on top allows air to enter.*

A mulch applied then is far more important than with spring-set plants when warm, favorable weather follows and plants start to make root and top growth. Before applying mulches to beds of perennials and bulbs, it is wise to let a frozen crust appear on the ground, as this prevents mice and other rodents from making warm and safe winter homes in the depth of the mulch. By then mice and other animal pests have already settled into winter quarters elsewhere.

Some mulches have already been mentioned, but it is a good idea to list as many as possible, since all kinds are not available everywhere—peat moss; compost; straw; marsh hay; shredded bark; wood chips; pine needles; buckwheat hulls; glass wool, which resembles cotton; cranberry branches; small and large leaves including those that curl, as oak; shredded leaves and brush trimmings; litter; polyethylene plastic, often placed around raspberries and other brambles or under other mulches to prevent weeds from growing through; and evergreen boughs. Save your old

Christmas tree, collect those of your neighbors, and better still obtain those not sold from local merchants. They are usually very happy if you take them away, as it will save them time and cost. Cut branches can be placed on the ground on top of perennials and bulbs or placed around small shrubs, with emphasis on evergreens, to keep off excess wind and sun.

Chrysanthemums need special winter mulching. It is not the cold that kills them so much as the uprooting when the freezing and thawing of the soil shoves the shallow, spreading roots upward during mild spells or winter thaws. To protect chrysanthemums, lift after flowering, allowing as much soil to cling to the roots as possible, and place them on the surface of the ground, along the side of the house, garage, stone wall, shed, or other structure, where they are protected from wintry blasts. Then when the soil freezes cover with a heavy blanket of a light material, chiefly marsh hay, straw, or evergreen branches. This method permits excellent root drainage—excess moisture and waterlogged soil are responsible for much winterkilling. Surprisingly, this technique will see plants safely through the most vigorous of winters.

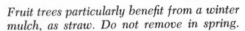

*Fruit trees particularly benefit from a winter mulch, as straw. Do not remove in spring.*

# 13

## Protecting Trees and Shrubs
## from Snow Breakage

WITHOUT A DOUBT the most important aspect of winterizing the garden is protecting trees and shrubs against breakage and splitting from the weight of snow and ice. Have you ever seen a tall, slender arborvitae snap in half from a too-heavy load of snow? Or the ground littered with the branches of white and other pines? Or a yew or boxwood hedge torn apart, an evergreen along the front of the house smashed to the ground from snow that slid off the roof?

Cleaning gutters from accumulations of leaves and debris will help prevent breakage to plantings along the foundations of houses. Remove clutter after the last leaves have fallen. To prevent annual cleaning out, place wire screening over gutters so leaves will not fall in. Handy home-owners can do this themselves, especially with ranch-style houses. With taller houses, employ a carpenter. The cost is worth it, and once done it will last many years.

I once designed a small city garden in which a large Japanese pieris, which then cost $35 without planting, was smashed by snow that fell from the roof in a winter of excessive snow. It had to be replaced at a cost of about $65 because the nurseryman came for it alone. After that, an attractive green frame was built and placed over it. The same snow sliding did not occur every winter afterward, but it did a few times, and the new pieris was saved. It happened to be located at a spot where wind piled snow at that point of the roof, and it was through experience and cost that the owners learned that the frame was needed to prevent the pieris from breaking again.

There was a time when gardeners would rake leaves from lawns, remove dead tops of perennials, pull up annuals killed by frosts, do a bit of haphazard pruning, and let it go at that, leaving the garden to the whims and vagaries of nature.

We now know better. Putting the garden to bed and especially pro-tecting trees and shrubs, the most valued plants in the garden, has become an art. More than anything else, the gardener realizes that the results can—and ought to—be attractive, not repulsive as they often were in the past.

Where snow slides off roofs, and it does just about everywhere, place wooden frames over the shrubs. You can make these frames yourself— boards or plywood cut to size, painted or left natural, and nailed to four stakes inserted around each specimen. Plants can receive sun and air, but when snow comes down with a sudden bang they do not break. These frames are easily taken apart in spring and stored in the basement or garage, where they take little space. Use them not only along foundations, but anywhere you have a prized rhododendron, azalea, boxwood, holly, or other shrub that you want to protect. So simple and so effective. In many instances it's that gardeners do not know about it.

*A simple and attractive method to protect large boxwoods and other evergreens is with two stakes, painted green or black, with rope tied all around.*

For tall evergreens as these arborvitae—apt to snap
in storms—vertical and horizontal supports are best.

Where snow may slide off the roof, pyramidal laths,
collapsible for storage, will solve the problem.

*Winter protection should be attractive. Burlap works well for evergreens, though this demonstrates what not to do.*

*Plants along house are protected from sliding snow with a lath and sheets of burlap to keep out wind and rays of sun.*

*This brick house is handsome, but not the method for handling evergreens, loosely tied with rope and pieces of burlap.*

*At the sides of a garage, strong boards painted dark green prevent snow piled by plow from breaking evergreens.*

*Evergreens along a house, badly smashed in previous winters, were tied with green twine. Photographed on December 2.*

*Same house on December 24, showing evergreens smothered with twenty inches of snow. Later eight more fell.*

*Photographed on February 20, when most of the snow had melted, evergreens came through the onslaught unbroken.*

*Individual yew to right of driveway showing how it was secured with soft green twine, which was barely visible.*

When snow from roof slid and broke a Japanese pieris to ground, it was replaced and this frame made for it.

Same Japanese pieris was protected for several winters with success. When neglected one winter this occurred.

*Oldest plant in the author's garden is this boxwood dating from 1933. It was covered every winter with sheets of burlap.*

*To protect boxwood, wooden stakes were inserted in the ground. Then several layers of burlap were secured with nails.*

*After winterized, this is how the boxwood, sheared each spring to control size, looked. The purpose of the stakes is to prevent boxwood from bending and breaking in snow.*

Better still are lath frames, often custom-made—sometimes with gables adding an architectural quality to your home. They have another advantage: sun and air pass through the openings at the tops, whether slanting or straight, yet they break the full brunt of snow that may fall on them. Lath frames are made so that they fold compactly and can be stored upright against a wall. If constructed of durable wood and treated with a preservative, they can be used over and over again. Redwood and cypress, expensive woods, do not need painting, as they will weather a beautiful gray. Other woods will need a coat of paint yearly, usually in the spring when they have been cleaned for storing or during the summer when not in use and you have time.

Another method of snow protection is to use boards or burlap along

*Boxwood in winter with heavy layer of snow. Without stakes it would bend over, as it did once. It did not break because snow was shaken from it whenever necessary.*

the sides of shrub plantings, not so much to prevent snow from falling on top, but to cut out sun and wind at the sides. This results in sunscald and windburning which shows up later in the burned, browned twigs and leaves on evergreens. Side protection is common along the seashore or in wide open spaces, including new housing developments where most of the large trees were cut down. Stakes are inserted in the soil and boards or sheets of burlap or polyethylene plastic are secured to them. If necessary, laths can be placed on the top, but not solid boards, as laths will let in sun and air while the boards will shut it out. Avoid covering plants entirely with polyethylene plastic, which gets too hot when the sun strikes it on mild days.

To eliminate plant breakage, insert a stake close to the center, like a

*Thirty-year-old Carolina rhododendron in author's garden, given another method of coverage, because snow piled from driveway at this spot would break it. Cover avoided this.*

tall óne used for dahlias, and tie branches to it with rope or heavy twine that will not cut. Start tying at the bottom, working upward in spiral fashion. Sometimes, two, three, or more stakes may be needed, but the results are always neat and attractive. With shrubs of questionable hardiness in your area, blue hydrangea or vitex in the North, for instance, go one step further. Wrap the plant with two or three layers of burlap, secured with long nails to act as hooks. In the case of blue or French hydrangea, forsythia, and lilac, this will prevent killing of flower buds produced on the old wood.

In some instances, and this applies mostly to large shrubs with strong stems, stakes will not be needed at all; simply the rope, twine, or soft string. Tying also succeeds with small shrubs, which may lean over with the weight of snow but will stand and grow upright again in the spring.

After four stakes are hammered in ground, a piece of plywood is nailed on top. In spring it was taken apart to be reused.

Protected Carolina rhododendron in winter with snow on top. Frame saved it from snow shoveled from driveway.

A simple way to handle an evergreen is to fasten it with string, tying at base and then winding it up spirally to the very top.

After tying with string, insert a single stake in center to support against snow, as with this convex-leaved holly.

Because of their small size and since they are tied in a bunch, danger of breakage is slight. Rather they are flexible, and just bend over. If completely covered with snow, so much the better, as it acts as a warm insulator.

A screen of boards, burlap, or polyethylene plastic is also recommended for plants near the street, including hedges, where snowplows can break them. Often the snow contains salt, as the streets are salted with sand while snow is falling or when it's icy, and then plowed later to clear them.

Protecting hedges along the front of the house by the sidewalk is of extreme importance. If you have unprotected evergreens like yew or convex-leaved holly, they may be spread apart by the weight of snow from the plow and never be able to regain their original shape. These protective screens also help prevent windburning, as they do shrubs in the foundation planting or anywhere in the garden. Stakes with strong wire stretched across will save hedges in places where traffic is light.

And, of course, do not forget to stake and brace trees, especially those recently planted, as wind and snow weight can break or cause them to fall over. Either individual strong metal or wooden stakes or guy wires can be used.

*Hidden stakes and branches of white pine secure these*
*hollies and euonymus from breakage, sun, and wind.*

# 14

## Decorate Window Boxes

FEW SIGHTS ARE MORE DREARY in winter than empty window boxes. In a sense, it's better not to set them up at all if you do not plan to decorate them and other permanent containers for the winter months.

Fortunately, more and more home gardeners are realizing the attractive possibilities for window boxes and other kinds of containers in winter. In the North, winter is the longest of the four seasons, cold and dismal, stretching from late October when summer plants are killed by frost until early May, when the first pansies, English daisies, and forget-me-nots can be planted.

In addition to window boxes, tubs and planters often adorn doorways. Concrete or metal urns if not planted with year-round evergreens look dull after the geraniums and chrysanthemums have been removed.

Just as container plants can do much to enliven your house and garden in summer, so they can do the same in winter in different yet attractive ways. Homeowners with facilities occasionally have two sets of boxes going, one for summer and one for winter. Winter boxes may be planted with small rooted evergreens, as yews, junipers, hollies, pieris, and camellias where weather permits.

The first step with window boxes and other permanent outdoor containers is to rid them of dead plant material, and give them a fresh coat of paint. Change their color for a different winter color scheme. Containers can be metal, and these too deserve a coat of paint. Do not paint concrete, as it is best left natural to weather and take on a soft gray.

Soil can remain in permanent outdoor containers three or four years. It does not have to be changed yearly. Each spring revitalize it with organic matter and fertilizer, applying heavy amounts as plants are set closely. Fall is a good time to take out old and put in new because you have more time. Do not, of course, add fertilizer as it will be wasted. Leave it for the spring planting of geraniums, marigolds, petunias, vinca, English ivy, and other plants.

If your window boxes are not lined with copper or zinc, consider it for

*Easiest way to decorate window boxes in winter is to insert plant material in soil before it freezes. Here balsam fir is used, highlighted with fruiting bittersweet and bayberry.*

it adds to their life considerably. This is especially recommended for those that are custom-built. The cost will be higher initially but less expensive in the end, plus you will not have to go through the bother of getting new boxes when the present have decayed and deteriorated.

What are the methods of fastening the greens, berries, and other materials? The most common is the soil itself. Boughs are simply inserted into the soil as deeply as possible, so wind will not dislodge or blow them out. When the soil freezes hard they are solidly anchored, and the severest blizzard cannot uproot them. For this reason you do not want to wait too long to decorate containers. In the North, Thanksgiving is just about the right time. Do not despair if a cold snap causes the soil to freeze as thaw generally follows early in the winter. If it does not, when you are ready to do the work soften by pouring boiling water over soil through a watering can or a pail.

A second aid, and one that helps prolong the life of the containers, is to remove the soil and place crumpled chicken wire inside, nailing it to the sides or along the top. Or tack a piece of chicken wire or wooden slats across the tops through which the stems of the greens and other plant materials can be inserted and held in place. Usually a little florist's wire is necessary to hold some of the stems firmly, and then the others will be supported by those already in place.

Another method is to set pieces of Styrofoam in the containers and insert the plants (which have been wired on florist's picks) in them. Better still, place a few large, heavy stones on the Styrofoam before decorating to make sure everything will stay in place in all kinds of winter weather.

As much as possible—if not entirely—rely on natural plant materials. There is such a wealth of it, some of it native, some imported from various parts of the country and even abroad.

Much material can be gathered from your garden as you do your early winter pruning. Yews, pines, and arborvitae in the North are all excellent, but the South provides English and other tender hollies, bull bay or southern magnolia, holly osmanthus, and cherry laurel. Avoid kinds of evergreens that shed. Two of these are hemlock and spruce, to be avoided entirely indoors where they last a matter of only days in a warm room. Outdoors, if cold, they keep longer, but after a while they drop their needles, especially if boxes are in sunny south exposures. However, if coated with the new Wilt-Pruf NCF, they will not shed.

Doubtless the most familiar and dependable green is balsam fir, native to the colder regions of the northeastern half of the United States and well into Canada. It may turn brown but never sheds outdoors or in. It is the typical "Christmas tree" of the East. With boughs of that alone you can adorn boxes so they will be green all winter, without going to the effort or expense to add plants with color. It is simple to do, and your boxes will not be drab.

Other kinds of evergreens make handsome displays—white, red, and Japanese black pines, as well as red, pitch, and Scotch. Junipers with gray-green leaves are excellent, but with these and others, you may want to add color. A well-decorated winter window box that is carefully planned can be as gay as a summer one.

What is brighter, for example, than dyed red ruscus, a plant with prickly leaves that is native to the Mediterranean regions? You can spot it a mile away, so to speak, and though some frown on it for its super gaiety, there are others who would not be without it. With lightly fallen snow, it is delightful and the color lasts all winter.

Two worthwhile berried plants are native bayberry and bittersweet. Unfortunately, birds will snatch the berries of the gray bayberry, so it is more recommended for the city gardener. The two make a classic combination, one used since colonial times, and the kind for a house a century

*This charming house would be more attractive had the window boxes been decorated for winter. Rather than leave them empty and forlorn, remove for winter if possible and store.*

or more in age. The Oriental bittersweet, which is yellow and orange, is sold frequently by florists. Another good fruiting plant is the bright red-berried black alder (*Ilex verticillata*), a deciduous holly. It keeps quite well through January and into February in the North, but not much longer. The same applies to broad-leaved hollies like American and English as leaves tend to scorch after a few weeks, quicker in sun than in shade.

Other fruiting plants include Washington thorn, a fine tree for the garden since its red berries not only last long but are not favored by the birds; orange Chinese lanterns; teasel, which may be natural or dyed red, orange, gold, or another color; love apples; California pepper berries; and especially straw-flowers—deep red, lavender, yellow, gold, orange, creamy-white—which have the odd habit of closing when wet by rain or snow and opening when dry, though they are dried.

Deciduous branches, as lilac, mock-orange, birch, shrub honeysuckles, and viburnums, can be silvered, gilded, or sprayed with "snow." Don't overlook the corky, winged twigs of the winged euonymus (*Euonymus alatus*), never failing to attract attention. If your taste is more conservative, these branches and twigs can be left in their natural state.

*If plastic containers crack when filled with soil in winter,*
*first insert crumpled chicken wire fastened with florist wire,*
*to which plant material can be tied or wired.*

There are many seed pods that can be gathered from the garden or the wild. If you let your bearded iris go to seed, use them for this purpose. Japanese tree lilac, sourwood or sorrel tree, and summersweet (*Clethra*) are all eligible. Among tropicals, lotus pods and wooden roses hold high esteem.

Douglas fir, pitch pines, Norway spruce, and the distinctive cedar of Lebanon have attractive cones that can be attached to greens with florist's wire and sprayed slightly with silver, not too much, just enough to simulate snow.

When plants in window boxes and other containers look beaten, dried up, and forlorn, usually in March and early April in the North, pull them out. That is the one period of lull, a few weeks before weather says go ahead with the planting of spring's first flowers—pansies, English daisies, forget-me-nots, wallflowers, and Dutch bulbs, which are sold in pots or flats just as they are coming into bloom. When that happens winter is over.

# 15

## Storing Tools, Equipment, Supplies, and Plants

Tools are the gardener's most valuable aids—without them he can accomplish very little. Fall, when the outdoor chores are finished, is the time to store them properly, although in winter when you have more time they can be given further attention so they will be ready for use immediately when spring comes.

Unhappily, too many gardeners do not take proper care of their tools. They falsely think that because they are not plants, and so not perishable, they will go on forever. In these days of high costs tools and equipment are a matter of sizable investments, worthy of the little care they need to keep them in top condition.

When such tools as shovels, spading forks, metal rakes, hoes, and spades will no longer be needed, clean off the soil (which, if left, will cause rust). It is advisable to wash them with a moist cloth or stiff brush, but then dry with a rag. If any rust is already present, remove with a paint scraper or steel wool, then oil or apply a rust preventer.

Next, clean and grease tools that cut, as pruning shears, loppers, saws, and tree pole pruners. If in need of sharpening, do it now, when your local mechanic and you have more time than in spring. He—or you if you are handy—can tighten any bolts or screws, then rub down handles with linseed oil to prolong their life.

Most difficult of all are the mechanical tools—the lawn mowers, rototillers, leaf shredders and blowers, and electric trimmers. Usually they require the attention of an expert, and this means sharpening and greasing parts to prevent rusting and corroding. Take them to a regular dealer, unless new, and when storing cover with old blankets or plastic to prevent dust from collecting. If a piece of equipment becomes broken, it may not mean a total loss as various parts can be replaced, making it as good as new. Using a chrome cleaner or grease solvent for certain mechanical equipment, particularly on the undersides as with mowers, will make machines look like new. However, if any tools or items of equip-

*Before storing hose for winter, it is important to empty it*
*of water by lifting at one end, allowing water to drain out.*

ment are beyond repair, it is better to buy new ones. Do it now when nursery and garden center attendants will have more time to explain the differences to you, and you may be able to make purchases at lower prices.

Other tools and pieces of equipment, mechanical or otherwise, that should be given attention just before storing or after they are placed in their final positions for the winter include electric- and battery-operated lawn edgers; sprayers, which should be washed with hot water and a detergent and then dried; dusters; hose reels; automatic water timers; sprinklers of all kinds; root feeders; hand shears; trimmers for hedges and edges of lawns; fertilizer spreaders; wheelbarrows and other carts used to haul soil and debris; and hoses.

The hose, rubber or plastic, is one of the gardener's most faithful and needed pieces of equipment. All too many people leave hoses in the hot sun on the lawn, where they deteriorate quickly. After using, if you do not have time to roll and place in the basement, garage, or tool house, do at least dump it in a heap in the shade of a tree or building—as the north side of the house or garage. This will prolong its life considerably. When the hose will no longer be needed, drain it completely of water, roll neatly, tie with string or rope, and hang on the side of the storage area, preferably cool and dry not damp and below freezing—true for all kinds of tools and equipment.

Give proper care to supplies—fertilizers, particularly chemical rather than organic, like dry manures, and chemicals of all kinds used for spraying insects and diseases. Be certain that all bags are closed and sealed with a piece of string or wire. If bags are torn, place in plastic bags. In the case of bottles and cans, make certain they are closed tightly, and if any have passed their deadline usefulness, as malathion which is volatile, toss out. Better to start with fresh stock in the spring if in doubt, rather than to go through the spraying procedure in vain—or possibly with harm.

Remember to bring soil from the garden to use for potting house plants in winter. Store in metal containers with covers or in plastic bags, kept tied. Sealing will keep most air out and retain the moisture in the soil. If allowed to dry out, valuable bacteria in the soil will be killed.

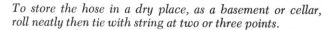

*To store the hose in a dry place, as a basement or cellar, roll neatly then tie with string at two or three points.*

*Statue of St. Francis and fantail pigeons, easy to lift, are wiped with moist cloth before storing in dry place.*

Some trellises are attached to the side of the house, garage, or fence and remain outdoors all winter, but others are for summer use only and should be taken in for the winter. Stakes of all kinds, whether tall wooden ones for dahlias, tomatoes, or pole beans, or bamboo or metal types for perennials and annuals, should be stored. First remove soil by scraping with a knife and then with a wet cloth. Dry, and if needed, give a coat of paint, unless you prefer to wait for winter, when you have more time.

Garden furniture, tables, chairs, benches, stools, and umbrellas also need proper storage. Wash with a sponge or moist cloth to remove dust and grime and then dry with a piece of cloth. Many statues and figures, small ones that are easily lifted, are best sheltered for the winter. Clean them in a similar manner, repair and patch as needed, and store, covering to keep off dust. Large statues that must remain outdoors can be protected with wooden frames placed over them to keep off snow and ice, as well as sun, which is damaging.

Where and how can all these items be stored? In a cool dry place where temperatures do not go below freezing. This is not always possi-

*Pedestal-type birdbaths should not be left out-of-doors
where winters are cold, but scrubbed before storing inside.*

ble, so you will have to make some compromises, determining which will
tolerate freezing and dampness and which will not. Use your common
sense and do not hesitate to ask friends and neighbors and consult agricultural experiment stations if in doubt.

Dryness is essential for chemical fertilizers and dusts, so place them on
shelves or blocks of wood to raise them above the floor that might be
damp. The average basement suffices for all storage but use ends farthest
away from the furnace. The old-fashioned cellar is equally good and
even better, because it stays somewhat cooler, invaluable for tender
bulbs and bottled or canned chemical sprays. These, incidentally, should
be kept in cabinets under lock and key if there are small children in the
household. Do not take any chances even if you feel your children are
old enough to know better.

Use your garage if the basement is not suitable. In colder parts of the
country, if the garage is unheated (and most are not) temperatures will
go below freezing and it will be damp. However, you can safely store
clay, plastic, and wooden pots; stakes and trellises and other painted
accessories (though a dry spot is better); sand for sidewalks, walks, and
driveways; and even tools if their metal parts have been oiled.

Bamboo stakes no longer needed should be gathered, cleaned with moist cloth, tied with Twist-ems.

To prevent pipes from freezing in winter, open faucet to drain. Basket stops water from making hole in soil.

Many people have tool houses, in which tools and supplies are kept in summer to make them handier to use. As a winter storage area, tool houses are more limited, because they are colder and damper than the garage, though this depends on the part of the country and winter temperatures. Above all, be certain they do not leak.

Do not neglect this aspect of garden care in the fall. With a minimum of effort and expense, you will be a more efficient gardener and will have a better garden with equipment that functions properly.

If you have a garden pool, it may need winterizing to prevent its sides from cracking or breaking. The easiest way is to float logs or large tree branches which act as cushions, preventing the pressure of freezing water from striking the sides of the pool. Another is to use unwanted metal buckets, pails, or large gallon drums, inverting them to hold air. When placed on the bottom and weighed down with large stones, expanding freezing water gently bends the sides of the containers inward, without breaking the sides of the pool, particularly concrete, inclined to break easiest.

A handy gardener's aid is the cold-frame. Basically, it consists of a box with a glass sash on top sloping in the direction of the sun to catch the

*Bring in garden soil for house plants in winter. Place in covered containers to keep soil moist and bacteria alive.*

*To prevent cracking or breaking, winterize concrete pools
with pails inserted upside down, held down with bricks.*

*Pool with pail immersed upside down in water, held in place
with eight bricks. Pails absorb pressure of freezing water.*

*A cold-frame is an ideal place to winter tender plants, as biennial English daisies, canterbury bells and pansies.*

warmth of its rays. The angle is necessary for rain and melting snow to roll off.

Any heat in the cold-frame comes from the sun. Wooden cold-frames, light and movable, are most common, although they can also be built of brick and cement blocks. In them daffodils, English daisies, forget-me-nots, hyacinths, pansies, tulips, violas, wallflowers, and other plants can be brought into bloom early.

In colder parts of the country it is essential to overwinter biennials, as canterbury bells, foxgloves, and sweet williams, in a cold-frame. Where not hardy, such plants as chrysanthemums, rosemary, and tritomas can be safely wintered in the cold-frame as well. Annual and vegetable seeds can be given an early start, and seedlings started indoors, like peppers, petunias, snapdragons, and zinnias, can be hardened off so they will not be injured from cold when planted in the garden after frost.

On warm spring days the sash on the cold-frame should be lifted, supported with one or two sticks to let in air and prevent overheating. Be certain to close at sundown if weather is cold, using reed mats or old quilts to cover afterward. If still cold, covers can stay on two, three, or more days, but take them off so plants can get sunshine when bitter weather is passed. As a rule cold-frames do not require frequent watering, especially not in winter as they are enclosed units that hold in moisture. Use your judgment about watering plants, lifting sashes on unusually warm spring days and watering lightly.

When a cold-frame is provided with heat it becomes a hotbed. The old-time method involves placing a layer of old manure at the bottom of the bed. Newer and more popular are hotbeds heated with electric bulbs which are expensive, or electric heating cables, less costly and easier to install. The cable is covered with plastic, making it resistant to corrosion, and is equipped with an automatic thermostat, assuring steady temperature.

Making a hotbed with cables is a complicated procedure for the average gardener. If you are bent on making your own, obtain specific instructions from library books or literature published by agricultural experiment stations or county agents.

The placement of the cold-frame or hotbed is important. The spot should be sheltered from winter wind, sunny for the greater part of the day. The south side of the house, garage, fence, or a hedge is best. Either should be filled with good soil, and sharp drainage is essential. With larger units, a one-foot-deep layer of crushed rock or coarse cinders is advisable.

Many kinds of seeds can be sown directly in the cold-frame or hotbed. Most need a temperature of seventy-two degrees to germinate, but young seedlings can withstand lower temperatures. Raising the sash lowers the temperature and helps to prevent damping-off disease, which causes seedlings to rot, wilt, and flop over at the base.

Watering is important, though plants or seedlings in cold-frames need water less often than those in hotbeds. Hotbeds full of plants may require daily moisture, and with either kind, water in the morning on a bright, sunny day so seedlings can dry off by nightfall. Never water late in the day.

If not inclined to making your own cold-frame or hotbed, ready-made units can be purchased. With hotbeds they come in sections with instructions so they can be put together easily. Once introduced to a cold-frame or hotbed, you'll find either or both indispensable to the success of your garden.

# Part Two

WINTER ACTIVITIES

# 1

## Shake Off Snow

SNOW ACCUMULATIONS on trees and shrubs, deciduous but particularly evergreens, are responsible for the greatest damage from breakage, spreading, and bending over (with tall kinds like arborvitae) of woody plants in winter. While true primarily of those uncovered or untied, it even can occur to those that have been given one form of protection or another, as staking a hedge of arborvitae, yew, or other evergreen.

Removal, if done as soon as possible, is a simple task. Just shake snow off small trees and shrubs with an old broom, a rake, a tall stake, or even a mop if it is the handiest item you can put your hands on. Long-handled shovels are also serviceable.

Evergreens, because they are still in leaf and because they tend to hold the snow, are the ones that suffer the most. Not only do they fall over, but they snap and break. Some spread apart, never to regain their forms again unless tied—formal hedges suffer the greatest toll in this respect. It's a sad sight to see an old hedge trained and pruned for years undergo this humiliation, but even sadder is the fact that it does not have to happen. A little foresight, know-how, and effort can prevent much misery and agony.

Shaking snow off small trees and shrubs of all kinds is not that difficult. It's a chore that a child can do and enjoy. What is essential is timing: if you do not do it when the snow is still soft, it may be too late. Whether powdery or wet, soft snow falls off easily, though wet snow is the kind to dread, as breakage might occur by the time you get to it.

In the case of a small storm, you can wait until it is over if it is still daylight. If night falls and you cannot work by street light, lampposts, or lights attached to the house, then do it before darkness sets in. This because you do not know what will happen during the night. If snow is the wet kind, it may freeze. It may snow again, or it may rain.

With an obvious blizzard you might need to shake snow two or three times during the day in order not to allow it to accumulate. Then if it continues to storm during the night, as it often does, you will have re-

*To prevent them from breaking, splitting, or spreading, use
an old broom or stick to shake snow from evergreens.*

moved some of the load. The more often you do it, the better.

One of the biggest dangers is snow that freezes. When it does, then
leave alone, otherwise branches may snap. Left undisturbed they stand a
chance of reviving, as they often do, even if somewhat spread apart, but
at least they can be tied back in place in spring. Large branches take a
long time to recover. Deciduous trees have great regenerative powers,
but not evergreens where gaps may never fill in.

The other threat—and it's worse—is encrustations of ice. You no doubt
have seen a litter of broken branches on the ground, the result of an ice
storm. All you can do is leave the trees or bushes entirely alone and hope
for the best. Hope that the next day will be milder, that the sun will melt
some of the snow. Hope that the wind will not blow, as plants covered
with snow or ice are less likely to break when they are still.

Plants that suffer most are those along the sidewalk at the front of the

*Each arborvitae in this formal hedge along a driveway was staked, yet this severe damage occurred after heavy snow. Damage could have been prevented if snow had been shaken.*

house or at driveways and walks, where shovels and plows are used to rid them of snow. A city plow can smash to pieces a yew hedge that is not braced; it can also be damaged by piling snow high on top of it. This is where snow removal with a bamboo rake, broom, or other piece of equipment is more than necessary.

The best advice is to keep the old broom, the rake, the tall dahlia stake at the front or back entrance, where they will act as reminders and be ready to use at a moment's notice.

To avoid injuring grass and low plants (as borders of pachistima and pachysandra) when removing snow with a shovel or plow along a driveway, insert wooden or metal stakes. Pound into the ground, a foot from the edge of the driveway, leaving tops about three feet tall. Also available are metal rods with round red heads that shine when car headlights strike them at night.

# 2

## Don't Use Salted Sand—
## Don't Tread on Lawns

Two EXTREMELY IMPORTANT "DON'TS" in preventing damage to plants in winter are much overlooked, almost entirely neglected. One is avoiding the use of salted sand on garden walks, driveways, and sidewalks, including near street trees. Though not an actual part of any garden, street trees are part of the overall landscape, and salted sand dumped on snow and ice along curbs and on sidewalks can damage street trees and plants along the front of the house. The other "don't" is not to tread on lawns, making regular paths as turf is often killed or weakened where walking is constant.

Few realize how much injury salted sand causes. Too much can be deadly, killing trees, shrubs, and other plants outright. In fact, salted sand has been causing so much controversy that many communities are forbidding the use of it, not only for trees, but because when snow melts, salt finds it way into drinking water, lakes, and reservoirs. Did you ever gather beach sand to use for pot plants? I once did as a boy, without realizing that salt is taboo, and all the plants died. I learned a lesson I never forgot. Hurricanes and other fierce winds along the ocean front will scorch and brown leaves of plants, and that is why seaside gardeners make a special effort to place boards along evergreens and other shrubs. When storms come during the growing season, as hurricanes in September, the best antidote is to hose down plants completely and let sprinklers run on lawns for several hours in order to leach as much salt as possible.

You can completely control the use of salted sand or rock salt in your garden. Use plain sand, which is effective, though without salt it does not melt snow and ice. Pour on plenty and keep adding more as it sinks in. No matter how much is applied, plants will not be harmed.

Around the house sand is needed on slippery sidewalks leading to all entrances. Here again, insist on plain, unadulterated sand. This applies to driveways bordered by lawns and flower borders. The most efficient

*Winter window box gay with red ruscus and balsam fir branches with pine cones is as attractive as any window box during spring to fall months.*

*Low container planted with pansies brings instant color before early plants start to flower in garden. Pansies bloom long in cool weather.*

*Chives and sages and other herbs grown indoors in winter can be set out in containers in spring where pieces can be taken to flavor food.*

Chinese hibiscus, single and double, in many colors, will bloom
all winter in warm parts of country. Veranda in Arizona garden
abounds in a wide assortment of foliage and flowering plants.

Dwarf dahlias in a bed, edged with a low hedge of santolina, bloom several months in California. Plantings in south Florida gardens require year-round care, even in winter when watering is essential.

Forsythia branches in author's home flowered in ten days when placed in water in a vase on the coffee table. Always cut branches in mild weather.

Snow fence on both sides of boxwood hedge along a driveway protects it from breaking when snow is plowed. Green-painted frames, which can be removed in spring and stored in summer, guard evergreens when snow slides from roof.

*Always use salt-free sand on garden walks and on sidewalks where plants adjoin, though several applications are needed.*

method is to keep pailfuls of sand at each doorway, with a tin, like a coffee can, or a bottle for scattering the sand on the walkway. As it empties refill immediately so it will be handy for the next time. In the fall make certain you have sufficient supply on hand, more than you think you will need.

To see the effects of salt on plants look at street trees in spring, where salted sand has been used regularly. The symptoms, interestingly, do not show up until after trees have leafed, usually in late spring or early summer in the northern parts of the country. Then leaves look as if they have been scorched, as they do during extended periods of summer droughts and excessive heat. Leaves are also small, curled, and stunted in growth. Trees that have been subjected to salt for years display other evidences —dead and dying branches at the top, leaves that turn color prematurely, in July and August, and a general lack of vigor. Eventually they die. Salt—sodium chloride—is that injurious, and overlarge intakes to the human body can cause much harm. We all know that persons suffering from heart disease, high blood pressure, and hardening of the arteries are allowed no salt at all in their diet, but we rarely relate salt damage to trees.

Trees usually affected are within thirty feet of the sides of roads and highways. For example, studies have shown that sugar maples—perhaps the most sensitive of all northern trees to salt—beyond thirty feet are healthy, while those closer to the sides of roads are increasingly affected.

*Red pine along highway showing dead branches and poor growth resulting from frequent applications of strongly salted sand.*

You can imagine what this means to plants in front of the house where snowplows shoot salted sand on evergreen hedges. Most sensitive of all is hemlock. A snow fence or siding of boards is a must if salt is used frequently where you live. Remember, too, that spray from passing vehicles is another factor that contributes its share of damage.

In the case of street trees, homeowners often purchase, plant, and care for their own, a common practice in cities. When making a selection, consider those that are more tolerant of salt than others. Very tolerant are red and white oak, both excellent shade trees. Also equally resistant are the native black cherry and red cedar, not street trees but for the front garden. You could choose gray, yellow, paper, and black birches, quaking aspen and large-toothed aspen. For street trees in this category, select white ash and black locust.

Moderately tolerant are red and Norway maples, basswood, shagbark hickory, spruces, and American elm, while least resistant of all—the ones to avoid where you know salt to be a problem—are hemlock, sugar maple, and red and white pines. So variable is salt tolerance to trees that a healthy Norway maple can absorb ten times as much salt as a healthy sugar maple.

The other problem, treading on lawns with snow and ice, is not so serious, but serious enough when you consider it is your own property. The most common issue is the short cut across the lawn. For this children are

*Avoid making regular paths on the lawn in winter especially when there is snow, as the compaction causes grass to die.*

the most guilty, when they find short routes to school and the local store. Years ago, the milkman was included, but not as much now, with supermarkets providing sources for most milk. The postman, then and today, is also to blame, and he must be watched. Walking over a lawn now and then is not harmful, but walking over the same area and creating a path will weaken turf or cause it to die. What happens is compaction, worse with snow and ice. When it occurs aerate in the early spring. Special tools are available, though a spading fork can be used, and be sure to reseed where necessary.

Easiest of all is to prevent it. If possible, talk to the individuals who make and use the paths, explaining why you do not want the practice continued on your own private property. If this does not work, you might have to build a fence or set out a hedge, an obstruction, worth the effort and cost if either fits well into your garden picture. Children who play over a large expanse of lawn do not cause damage since they are not treading the same areas constantly. With small lawns regular playing should be avoided.

If these suggestions are not practical, another hindrance is to set up a temporary wire or other fence obstruction for the winter only. Often two or three stretches of rope secured to strong stakes will suffice, a solution that is quick, easy, and inexpensive. Sometimes signs help, a yet easier way, but in any case give your lawn the winter care it needs, as tramping causes snow mold and winterkilling. As it is, lawns undergo enough setbacks on their own, what with ice and other uncontrollable actions of winter weather.

# 3

## Apply Anti-desiccant Sprays

MUCH OF THE WINTER DAMAGE that occurs on trees and shrubs, notably evergreens, actually goes on behind the scenes. Unlike bending and breakage, it is not visible, but shows up in late spring and early summer. The main danger is from windburning, a term often used but little understood.

During winter trees, shrubs, and vines continue to absorb and give off water, at a higher percentage when winds are strong and the sun bright. If the ground is not frozen, as is often the case, water loss is replaced by moisture in the ground, though often not to the extent needed if sun and wind are excessively drying.

When moisture is no longer available, either because of dryness or frozen soil, leaves and stems still continue to transpire, even taking moisture from living cells. What happens then? Desiccation or drying out (windburn), resulting in browning or actual killing of leaves and stems, which does not show up until May or June when plants have made new growth.

It is not rare to then see yews with dead branches, usually referred to as dieback, which have to be removed. English boxwood, where not totally hardy, may die nearly to the ground. In June rhododendrons resplendent with bloom and new lush growth may sport dead brown branches with curled leaves that droop downward, unsightly if not cut off. In various parts of the country, depending on climate and plant material, desiccation occurs in varying ways and degrees, worse in some winters than in others.

Broad-leaved evergreens, like hollies, leucothoes, mahonias, mountain laurels, and rhododendrons, suffer most because they possess large leaf surfaces that are exposed to sun and wind. Another factor that makes for greater injury is snow, not its weight that breaks branches, but the reflection of the sun's rays on the pure white of snow. In late February and March, when sun is higher in the sky and days are longer, damage is greater because of its warmth and intensity.

What can be done to prevent windburn? The answer is simple and the

*An anti-desiccant spray in easy-to-use pressurized bomb will
prevent windburning after applied to evergreens in the fall.*

effort, along with cost, minimal: apply a liquid latex spray. This forms a
plastic coating on stems and leaves so transpiration is reduced. At the
same time, leaves can give off water, as they should, while maintaining a
proper balance with the moisture-absorbing capacity of the roots.

These plastic sprays are not new, and there have been varying opin-
ions among experts about their lasting effectiveness. I have used them
often with much success. It's all a matter of following directions carefully, as it is with fertilizers and chemical sprays to control pests and diseases where timing is of extreme importance. Instructions are given for a
good reason and should be heeded in all garden activities but more
where chemicals are involved.

First to appear on the market, nearly twenty years ago, was Wilt-Pruf,
but others are available under such names as Stop-Wilt, Foli-gard,
D-Wax, Folicote, Plant-cote, and Good-rite Latex VL-6000. Wilt-Pruf has
now come out with a new, improved formula known as Wilt-Pruf NCF,
described as "100% organic . . . and approved for use on all growing edible crops and raw agricultural commodities." Unlike the former product
and others, which were best applied twice for a more lasting effect—
once in the late fall or early winter and again in late February or March
—two sprayings in the fall, an hour apart, will suffice.

What is the general step-by-step procedure for using anti-desiccant sprays? Choose a mild, sunny day, usually in November or early December, when the temperature is well above 40° F., as you cannot get an effective plastic film if readings are lower. The same temperature is necessary if using a kind that should be applied again in late winter or early spring, when dehydrating winds coupled with snow and sun are fierce.

For a few plants the spray can be applied with an aerosol bomb, but for larger areas mix in a sprayer according to directions. With Wilt-Pruf NCF the proportion is five parts water to one of plastic. Make certain the sprayer is clean, and one with a fine mist is better and less wasteful than a spray that is coarse. Above all, clean the sprayer after using, before the plastic hardens, with warm water and a common household detergent.

Plastic sprays have other uses. They can be applied to evergreens and other woody plants that are planted in the late fall or early spring. Since leaves and stems are coated, transpiration caused by wind and sun is slowed down, making it possible to set out and transplant plants as long as the ground is frozen. Plastic sprays can take the place of burlap, boards, and other mechanical coverings, provided there is no danger of breakage. Without these props, plants keep their natural beauty all winter long.

*Windburning on well-established rhododendrons where an anti-desiccant spray was not used. Be sure to remove dead growth in spring.*

*Rhododendron photographed at 26 degrees F. shows upper*
*left leaves thawed by sun, while those in shade remain frozen.*

Wilt-Pruf NCF possesses other virtues. It helps guard plants against the ill effects of air pollution; the protective film, which is transparent, does not allow soot and grime to attack evergreens and other plants in city gardens. It helps ward off other toxic materials, as salt spray common in seaside gardens and urine from dogs.

You can apply it to Christmas trees so they will last longer indoors. Types like spruce that shed will not drop their needles. If you want a potted live Christmas tree, becoming more and more the trend, spray with the plastic (one part plastic to ten parts water) before taking indoors to lessen drying out. In turn, the live Christmas tree in a container will undergo less of a shock if placed outdoors, in parts of the country where weather permits, or put in a cool place, as garage, breezeway, entranceway, or unheated room, until ready for planting outdoors in spring.

Like other garden chemical products, plastic sprays should not be stored where it is too hot in summer, above 120° F. or below freezing in winter. Though the new Wilt-Pruf NCF can be kept for two years, it is better to use within nine or ten months after purchasing.

Whether using the handy aerosol dispenser or mixing your own in sprayers, remember one very important point: do not apply when temperatures fall below 40° F. Not that harm will follow, but the water will freeze, especially if the temperature is considerably lower, and evaporate slowly, resulting in a coating of ice, which is hardly beneficial to plants and will result in some breakage among small, delicate evergreens.

# 4

## Ideal Pruning Time

MILD, SUNNY WINTER DAYS are perfect for pruning trees, shrubs, and vines, both evergreen and deciduous. Without foliage on deciduous woody plants, it is easier to see what you are doing, to give the trees, shrubs, and vines the forms and shapes you want. Early pruning induces the development of latent buds, which grow vigorously to fill in holes, conceal ugly cuts and wounds, and give each plant the natural, graceful character that is its own.

The main idea of pruning is to control growth, to restrict it, so one plant does not crowd out another, yet maintain the lovely form of each kind (clipping and shearing, as found in formal gardens, are not pruning). Unless checked, woody plants become too large and lanky for their locations, and good pruning requires skill and know-how. Among gardeners it is considered an art, one that improves with experience.

Through judicious or natural pruning you "open up" each tree or shrub to let in more air and sun, freeing centers to increase circulation. Cutting lower branches on trees will also help achieve this. First remove dead or weak wood. Cut branches that are too dense or rub or cross each other, and any others you feel will improve the overall appearance. V-shaped crotches, which split easily in winter and summer storms, are undesirable so remove one branch, thus eliminating this danger. Shorten extra-long branches and shoots of trees and shrubs. When it comes to pruning, there is no one "correct" way, but follow the simple, basic rules and suggestions and then use your best judgment.

The equipment you use is very important. For small branches, particularly shrubs, pruning shears are handy. They will make small cuts, but be certain the shears are sharp. When pruning thorny bushes, as five-leaf aralia or pyracantha, use gloves. One group of plants not to touch is roses. Even fall pruning is minimal. Leave just about all rose pruning in the North for early spring.

Loppers have long handles—their purpose is to cut larger and heavier branches up to one-and-a-quarter inches in diameter. They have good

*Thirty-year-old jetbead in the author's garden showing vigorous growth after its annual pruning. Additional series of pruning photographs appear on pages 142-3.*

leverage and enable you to reach into thick, impenetrable growth in shrubs, including those that have been neglected for years.

To reach higher—eight, ten, fifteen, or more feet—you will need tree or pole pruners. You can operate them standing on the ground or from a sturdy ladder. They rarely cut branches more than an inch in diameter, but are excellent for small outer branches and twigs, extra-long shoots, and suckers at the base of trees, characteristic of crab apples, lindens, and maples. Suckers are shoots that appear at the bases of plants, as lilacs, which are not grafted. They may also show up on plants like roses, crab apples, and Oriental cherries below the point of graft. In that case, it is important to keep cutting them off as the vigorous rootstock will take over. When it comes to reaching higher than standing on the rung of a tall ladder, do not take a chance, as it involves a liability—not worth taking the risks. Engage professional arborists who are skilled and insured.

*Thirty-year-old dwarf winged euonymus before pruning in late winter, before leaf and flower buds began swelling.*

*Pruning the dwarf winged euonymus. The branches were cut at varying lengths in order to maintain a natural appearance.*

*Dwarf winged euonymus on July 8, after the new growth had developed. Notice the open, non-sheared character.*

There are many kinds of saws to use in pruning, and each does a different job. Some will cut suckers at the base, others side branches along the trunks of trees. Some have teeth—different sizes—on both sides of the blades. Two-handled saws are useful for two persons to cut extra thick branches. It is a good policy to keep as many different kinds of saws in your storage area as your trees and shrubs will require. Learning what each can and cannot do is of vital importance.

When you prune, make a neat flush cut back to another branch, being careful not to rip off bark. This is more apt to happen with a large branch, so support it until it is severed completely. With very large branches, cut in sections. Always avoid stubs, that is, pieces of branches not cut flush at points of origin. They are unsightly and permit the entrance of fungus diseases and insects—a reason you must cover cuts an inch or more in diameter with tree-wound paint. It acts as a sealer that keeps out moisture as well. Use an aerosol bomb for small cuts, but for a great amount of pruning use a can and brush (clean in turpentine and then wash in hot water with soap), the size depending on the cut.

Some trees "bleed," or lose sap if pruned freely, especially as early spring advances. This accounts for the tapping of sugar maples in March in the northern parts of the Northeast, providing syrup for pancakes. These "bleeders," the ones you should avoid pruning at least vigorously, include beeches, birches, hornbeams, magnolias, maples, tulip trees, wal-

Large oak with small low branches with weed hickory at the base before pruned in late winter. Purpose of pruning was to "lift up" the tree and display the trunk to advantage.

When removing branches from trees or shrubs, do not leave stubs. They are unattractive and will eventually decay, inviting diseases. Always seal cuts with wound paint.

When removing lower branches from a tree, use a ladder but do not try dangerous climbing. Engage an arborist. Several kinds of saws can be used, depending on the size of the branch. Tools must be sharp.

Weed hickory was removed with hand loppers and a saw, which cut the trunks flush with the ground. Branches can be cut in pieces, cured in a dry place, and used to burn in fireplace.

To thwart weed hickory from sprouting at base, make gashes with an ax and pour gasoline or weed-killer, as 2,4,-5-T, on top. Once usually is enough, but if sprouts show up it can be done a second and last time.

Oak after it was pruned and the new growth had fully developed, shown photographed on June 23. Later some lower branches on the oak at the left were cut off to make the two trees symmetrical.

nuts, and yellow-wood. The time to prune them, when they do not bleed, is late summer or early fall. However, there is little harm if pruning is not drastic, and certainly you will want to get rid of dead and weak branches.

With vines it is important to do some pruning each year, with emphasis on twining kinds like actinidia, bittersweet, Dutchman's pipe, and wisteria (prune clematis in early spring, not winter) to control tangled masses of growth. If in doubt about the pruning of vines, wait for early spring when buds begin to swell, but go light on wisterias as too heavy pruning will do away with flower buds. Wait until after flowering to do the big cleanup job. This applies to several flowering spring shrubs, among them burkwood and mayflower viburnums, Cornelian-cherry, February daphne, spireas, and witch-hazels.

With shrubs—and whether trees or shrubs, prune only very hardy kinds—cut a few of the oldest branches directly to the ground. This will keep them vigorous and "young," stimulating new branches from the base to replace the old that eventually lose their strength and flower sparingly. Unless very hardy in your area, leave summer-flowering shrubs (butterfly bush, rose of sharon, and vitex) for the spring, as cold winter weather will do an enormous amount of "pruning" whether you realize it or not.

*Jetbead by author's garden gate before pruned on April 5.*
*Early pruning is needed in order to stimulate latent buds.*

When pruning cut one-third of oldest branches directly to ground, as this results in new, vigorous growth from base.

Jetbead as it appeared after pruned on April 15. Drastic cutting is essential as bed is narrow, a few feet wide.

# 5

## Feeding the Winter Birds

BIRD WATCHING has become a national pastime—as has feeding, mostly in winter when food is scarce. In winter new interest is added when different birds, such as evening grosbeaks, juncos, and redpolls, migrate from other parts of the continent.

Once in the habit of frequenting feeders, birds, including year-round residents, migratory species, and winter visitors, always go to them for food. If you derive pleasure from watching birds, consider installing a feeder in your yard, perhaps at the kitchen window. You will be helping the birds find food when there may be little in their natural environment.

The feeder may be simply a piece of wood with the bark left on. Highly recommended are feeders on poles that move with the wind so openings do not face prevailing winds. A baffle below helps discourage squirrels and other animal pests, including cats. Keep feeders well supplied since birds seek others if one is continually empty. On the other hand, do not overstock unless you are eager to attract a new species, as too much food will only encourage the undesirable types—notably starlings and English sparrows.

Even starlings have their virtues, however. They are enormous devourers of insects in summer, and their exceptionally keen eyesight will not allow the tiniest bug to escape, including ants which they eat in quantities. If the much maligned English sparrow has one attribute, it is his penchant for Japanese beetles.

Most feeders are stocked with seed, and wild bird seed is inexpensive and available everywhere. Birds have their preferences so include as many kinds as possible, adding rape, flax, and niger to wild mixtures to attract goldfinches, purple finches, and pine siskins, winter residents in the North. Robins, sometimes stragglers in the North, and catbirds are fond of raisins and pieces of apple, and suet is a favorite with nuthatches and hairy woodpeckers.

Avoid peanut butter as it can be harmful, sticking to the roofs of

*Keep bird feeders well stocked with food all year round.*
*Otherwise birds will leave your garden for other feeders.*

mouths of birds like chickadees, who choke to death trying to dislodge it. When seed-eating birds eat too much peanut butter they lose the gravel in the gizzard so it fails to function properly, causing enlargement of the liver.

You can see and enjoy birds more in winter when trees and shrubs are leafless. Try to place feeders near trees so birds can alight to look out for enemies before heading for their meals. If pests become a problem for birds on your property, get in touch with a local game warden for methods of control.

Installing feeders is not the only way to draw winter birds to your garden. Another is to supply them with water, or plant trees and shrubs that bear edible fruits. Because of feeders and increased plantings of fruiting

*One of the best ways to attract birds to your garden is by planting fruiting trees and shrubs, as crab apples.*

trees and shrubs on a national scale, many birds from the South have wandered North or have stayed in the North all winter, among them mockingbirds and cardinals. With their stomachs well-packed with food, they are better able to withstand the rigors of northern winters.

Some early berry trees and shrubs that supply food during the summer include February daphne, doublefile viburnum, and shrub honeysuckles. Others that follow include aronias, bayberry, bittersweet, crab apples, dogwoods, hawthorns, junipers, shadbushes, and all kinds of viburnums. Bayberry is a favorite of the migratory myrtle warbler.

Some fruits are not eaten by birds until midwinter or early spring, either because they are sour or too large, as the Siberian crab apple, and can be eaten only after they have been broken down by frost action. Barberries, privets, sea-buckthorn, Washington thorn, and others have saved the lives of many birds in sudden spring snowstorms. In fact, I have often seen pigeons, non-perching birds, alight on privets to eat the black berries in cold midwinter when food is scarce.

Two other methods for feeding birds in winter are equally simple. One is to allow flowers of many perennials and annuals to go to seed, among them coreopsis, cosmos, rudbeckias, and sunflowers, a favorite. The other is to scatter handfuls of bread crumbs, perhaps the easiest practice of all.

# 6

## Bringing the Outdoors Indoors in Winter

THERE ARE MANY lovely ways to bring the outdoors in during midwinter. One is by gathering greens of various kinds and placing them in water in vases and other containers throughout the house where they will last several weeks, some even months. The other is to gather branches of flowering trees and shrubs, as Chinese witch-hazel and forsythia, and force them into bloom indoors.

Every garden has some evergreen trees and shrubs. Most keep well for a long time in water with a few exceptions, notably spruces and hemlocks which shed their needles after a while. They last longer in water than out, and that alone may suffice for a party or special occasion. Through experience you learn which keep and which do not, but mostly it's a matter of utilizing what you grow in your garden.

Greens add life and warmth to interiors, as they do outdoors in winter when deciduous trees and shrubs have shed their leaves. They take the place of foliage house plants and cost nothing. Just as many gardeners wait until near Christmas to "prune" their evergreens (to use the cuttings and boughs for decoration indoors), so they can do the same in midwinter, after the holiday season is past. Then they are needed even more, after the Christmas tree and other colorful ornaments have been taken down. Thus, you do two things: you prune, and you decorate the rooms of your home with living green.

What do you need? Sharp pruning shears, as most branches taken will vary from one to three feet in length. If you want boxwood or yew snippets to decorate the dining-room table when you have guests, or for small vases placed around the house, sharp scissors will do. Occasionally you might want to take very large branches for a special occasion, so a saw will be needed. When you cut be certain that the evergreens can take this kind of severe cutting.

Next in importance is when to cut, for in cold areas, with much below-freezing weather, cutting can be done only when the thermometer is above the freezing mark—during mild spells when branches are firm and

*Forsythia branches force easily in water if gathered on a warm day, particularly after rain. Long branches are best. They can be cut into smaller ones later for small bouquets.*

full of sap. Have you noticed how rhododendron leaves curl and droop when temperatures are in the twenties? They do this to expose less leaf surface to the sun and wind and thus cut down on transpiration. Taken then, leaves revive but lack sufficient sap to regain their luster and last a long time. A mild spell or thaw is an excellent time to cut rhododendrons, but best of all is a warm spell accompanied by rain. You can cut during or just after the rain, before freezing weather sets in again.

In many cases, it is helpful to place a pin holder at the bottom of the container you use, secured with clay, in which two or three of the largest branches are inserted. These act as a base, and the others can be arranged around them. Either fill with water part way as you start to arrange or pour water after the work is done. You can add pieces of broken charcoal, the kind recommended for potting mixtures, as this helps keep the water pure.

Add water as it evaporates. Some cuttings, as florist "lemon leaves" (*Gaultheria shallon*), whose correct common name is shallon or salal,

*Forsythia branches in a vase with water can be placed any-where, not necessary at a window. Cut them from early January onward, and buds will start to open in a week.*

and rhododendrons, will keep so long they need dusting. Remove the branches about once a month, scrub the inside of the container with a stiff brush and a detergent to get rid of scum and algae, more prevalent if charcoal is not used. Change the water, add some new charcoal (keep the old), and make fresh cuts, splitting thick, woody stems down the center with a sharp knife so they will draw water more easily. This should also be done at the start. Then rearrange, perhaps adding some new branches, a different kind for foliage size and leaf texture.

A cool entranceway is a good place to use cut greens, for they will last longer. Needless to say, greens do not require much light and will keep better out of direct sun. Large containers with tall branches can be placed on the floor or a low stool, often in a corner where little else can be used. If you do not have a garden, you can still enjoy the green of outdoors by buying greens from florists. The already mentioned "lemon leaves" is one of the most common, often appearing in florist bouquets. Another is huckleberry, as florists term it, but is truly box-huckleberry

(*Gaylussacia brachycera*), with small, oval, shiny, one-inch long leaves. Like "lemon leaves," it is often used in florist bouquets as backing.

Remember that bare branches in themselves can be attractive, as well as plants whose berries last well into the winter, like bayberry, bittersweet, firethorn or pyracantha, Siberian crab apple, and Washington thorn. Seed pods of summersweet or clethra, Japanese tree lilac, jetbead, and sourwood, and others can be put to use.

Among the best greens that grow in the cold North are American holly, arborvitae, boxwoods, chamaecyparis, convex-leaved Japanese holly, evergreen azaleas, hardy bamboos, inkberry (*Ilex glabra*), junipers, mahonias, mountain and Japanese pieris, pines, and rhododendrons.

In warmer parts of the country your selection is enlarged to include abelia, arbutus, bamboos, berried ardisia, boxwoods, camellias, cherry laurel, Chinese sacred bamboo, cryptomeria, English, Chinese, and other hollies, Japanese aucuba, Japanese euonymus, Japanese privet, large-leaved bull bay, the counterpart of rhododendrons in the North, rosemary for fragrance, southern pines, and yews.

The second method of bringing the outdoors in involves color. By cutting flowering branches at the right time, when weather is mild, you do not have to wait for spring but can enjoy it in advance from blossoms of flowering trees and shrubs. Forcing them is just as easy as forcing paper white narcissus in pebbles and water, growing lentils, and aglaonema or philodendron in water for indoor green.

In addition to cutting in warm weather—best after a gentle rain—and using sharp tools, timing is very important. Do not start too early, but wait for cold weather to "mature" flower buds. The best time is after Christmas, and if there have been some cold snaps, you can start with forsythia—the most common and the easiest—in the middle of January. The longer you wait—the closer to outdoor flowering time—the better the results.

Weather is even more important than with greens since you are interested in blooms. Branches must be full of sap, the more the better. Ones cut on a cold, bitter day when the thermometer registers ten degrees or so lack sap and are brittle and snap easily.

February and March in the North present the best weather. If possible take large branches because they contain more sap. As flower buds swell you can cut smaller branches to arrange for coffee tables, mantels, side tables, bookcases, dining-room tables, or simply for a floor vase.

An advisable step, again if space and facilities permit: immerse branches in a large basin of water or, better still, the bathtub overnight to soften the hard covering over each flowering bud, particularly needed by some kinds, as flowering dogwood and saucer magnolia. Generally, the sooner the flowering tree or shrub blooms outdoors, the easier it is to force, as February daphne, forsythia, and Korean azalea.

*Greens make lovely decorations indoors in the middle of winter. Rhododendrons last fully two months.*

*Prune evergreens—like yew, juniper, convex-leaved holly—at Christmas by taking cuttings for the holidays.*

Branches with fat, rounded buds give the most bloom. Those that are pointed and slender usually develop into leaves. Plants that are growing in full sun tend to produce more flower buds than those in shade. Splitting large stems or crushing them with a hammer results in quicker and better water intake, thus superior flowering.

At the start branches do not need light, but will as buds begin to break. Give them some sun and flowering will be better, the colors of the flowers deeper. If you can force in a cool place, growth will be slower and flowers will last longer. Always keep away from direct heat, especially radiators or baseboards. Keep adding water as it evaporates, change it from time to time if you wish, though it is not necessary as these blooms only last a few weeks. Again, adding crushed charcoal will help keep water free of algae.

First to "flower" are pussy willow, either the wild or the cultivated hybrids with their fat pinkish catkins. So start with these, then shift to forsythia. What could be more cheerful than a vase of golden forsythia on a day when a blizzard is raging outside? Forsythias do not need sun or light—merely place them where you will want them to perform. Surprisingly, even without flowers the branches will be attractive, as somehow branches "arrange" themselves much more easily than cut flowers.

Then follows a long line of early-flowering trees and shrubs—February daphne, in rose-lavender or white, with tiny, sweetly scented blossoms; Chinese witch-hazel, with fragrant yellow flowers, excellent to combine with a few florist's daffodils and a few sprays of green from the garden; vernal witch-hazel, with red-yellow flowers.

The small white flowers of winter honeysuckle give off an enchanting fragrance, remindful of spring. Try the yellow Cornelian-cherry, with yellow blossoms; crab apples; flowering dogwoods; Japanese flowering quince in many colors; kerria with green stems and single or double golden blossoms; lavender Korean azalea; mayflower and burkwood viburnums; Oriental cherries in pink and white; wild white shadbushes; and yellow spicebush.

Fruits, as apple, apricot, cherry, peach, and pear, flower well; better if taken in late winter. The red flower clusters of the native red maple need not be overlooked; nor catkins of aspens, birches, speckled alder, common in wet places; and simply the small, expanding bright green leaves of horse chestnut or tulip tree.

Oddly enough, the early-flowering saucer magnolia (*Magnolia soulangeana*) is one of the most difficult to force, but do not hesitate to give it a try. To succeed will be rewarding in itself. Take as large branches as possible and soak for several hours (this is absolutely necessary) in the bathtub in warm water to soften the furry, coated coverings that protect the flower buds from winter's cold.

# 7

## Check Bulbs in Storage

MANY GARDENERS lose their tender bulbs, like caladiums, dahlias, and tuberous begonias, in winter because they neglect them or do not know how to give them the right care. Storing tender (and what is tender varies with the part of the country) bulbs is not simply a matter of digging and placing them in a medium in the basement, cellar, or a closet for the winter. You should check them periodically—as often as twice a month—to see if they are rotting, shriveling, or deteriorating in one way or another.

Rotting usually results from disease or keeping the medium—as peat moss or soil—too moist. Shriveling is caused by dryness, and the problem with storing bulbs nowadays is that basements, compared to the cool old-fashioned cellars, are too warm and dry. Deterioration may be due to either of these factors, or temperatures that are too cool. When storing tender bulbs, learn the average temperature at which they should be kept and then do the best you can according to available facilities. If you do not have proper requirements, one possibility is to give bulbs to friends to keep for you.

Shriveling from too much dryness is the most common occurrence. Present-day basements, well insulated, are hot and dry, and the garage is no place to store tender bulbs if temperatures go below freezing. However, if your garage gets some heat, so that the thermometer in the coldest weather stays well above freezing, it is often an ideal place since it is cooler than the basement, and coolness is what most bulbs need.

When you check bulbs (cannas, dahlias, tigridias, and tuberous begonias stored in peat moss, sand, soil, vermiculite, or perlite) and find they are shriveling, simply sprinkle with water, just enough to revive them and make plump again. Be careful not to give too much water, which may cause rotting. If kept warmer than required, as they often are, they will still keep well if the matter of watering now and then is not forgotten.

*Examine dahlias and other bulbs in storage periodically. If shriveled sprinkle with tepid water to make turgid again.*

To determine if bulbs are shriveling, it may be necessary to take them out of their boxes, cartons, or other containers, though sometimes inserting your hand deep into the medium is enough for you to check their condition. Nowadays bulbs are kept in plastic bags, secured at the top to keep out air (plastic bags allow some air to enter through the sides), and these need checking just as well. If showing signs of wrinkling, then sprinkle on the basement floor and when mostly dry, place in the plastic bags again, tying openings as before with string or Twist-ems.

Next look for rotting, usually caused by diseases present on the bulbs when dug and stored, though it is often impossible to determine at the time. Needless to say, if some are badly rotted, throw them away. They are hopeless and retaining portions will only infest others in the same containers. Often rotting is minimal, as a tuber or two on a clump of dahlias, and in that case cut out the diseased portions with a sharp knife and dust the rest with sulphur to kill disease spores that are present on the bulbs. Rotting may also be caused by keeping bulbs too moist, in which case the same treatment should be followed. Be careful not to wet too often and keep too moist.

In addition to storing tender bulbs in proper medium and place, get to know the temperature requirements of each kind. For example, dahlias and gladiolus can withstand considerable cold. In storage, they both like readings between 35° F. and 40° F. Proper storage temperatures for other much-grown tender bulbs are as follows: 40° F. to 50° F. for calla-lilies, cannas, montbretias, and tigridias; 50° F. to 55° F. for the dainty achimenes—generally grown in hanging containers and window boxes—Peruvian daffodil (*Hymenocallis*), and tuberous begonias; 60° F. to 65° F. for tropical caladiums and tuberoses, which as a rule do not flower well a second year, so it is advisable to purchase new bulbs.

If you prefer earlier bloom, start bulbs indoors from February to March, depending on your climate, in large pots, flats, or other containers. Bulbs to start this way include caladiums, cannas, dahlias, tuberoses, and tuberous begonias. This head start can make quite a difference, as you'll get bloom much sooner than from bulbs set directly in the open ground once all danger of frost has passed.

If you have Dutch bulbs—crocus, daffodils, hyacinths, and tulips—you were unable to plant in the fall, keep in bags in as cool a spot as possible. Then plant in the garden in the early spring as soon as the ground is workable. Do not wait until fall as they will deteriorate and shrivel and often die. In the ground they will revive, make roots when the right time comes, and bloom the following spring. Keeping them out of the ground is harmful. After all, they stay in the soil all year around, through wet and dry periods, through flowering and dormancy.

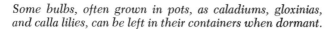

*Some bulbs, often grown in pots, as caladiums, gloxinias, and calla lilies, can be left in their containers when dormant.*

# 8

## Keep Busy Indoors

NEARLY ALL WINTER chores can be lumped under the head of keeping busy indoors, and though some can be done in late fall or early spring, many can be crossed off your list if performed in midwinter, when you are apt to be less busy.

If, for example, you did not get your tools with working parts in good order when stored, do it now. Clean them with a piece of stick, wash with a moist cloth, and then dry. Rust can be removed with steel wool or a rust remover, followed by a protective coating of grease or wax, including ordinary floor wax. A cheap grade of vaseline can be substituted, though other materials are also available.

Equally important, make certain tools with cutting parts are sharpened. Have it done now so they will be in good working order when needed in spring. These tools include lawn mowers, both mechanical (from which gasoline must be removed) and hand; pruning shears; pole pruners; grass shears; loppers; and electric- and hand-operated hedge trimmers, along with shredders and leaf blowers. Then examine, clean, and oil other tools, as shovels, spading forks, spades, and rakes, especially if neglected at storage time.

Sprayers are in a category by themselves—among the most important and yet delicate tools, apt to clog and not operate, especially when you've prepared the spray materials and are ready to go ahead. It is hard to imagine anything more frustrating. Sprayers should always be washed out thoroughly. Use rust removers in the case of galvanized types. All need to be stored in a dry place. Replace washers, and to forestall all detrimental rust, apply oil to wheels of fertilizer spreaders and other tools with movable parts.

No matter where kept, snow blowers will need attention, more so if they are in frequent use. Care is similar to lawn mowers, except that it is more constant. Keep spare parts on hand and learn how to replace worn-out ones. If possible, have two snow blowers on hand, in the event one fails to work in the midst of a blizzard.

*Spraying house plants for pests, as red spider mites, scale, and mealy bugs, requires all-winter attention. An aerosol bomb is handy, but read directions carefully.*

Next comes painting: trellises, tables, chairs and stools, tubs, window boxes and other containers, and stakes. Terrace furniture, including removable benches, may need repairing, but if unable to do it yourself, employ a carpenter or other handyman. If you have the skill—and the necessary tools and equipment—you may want to make these items, including birdhouses and shelters. These should not be painted, but left to weather naturally once placed in position in early spring. Make or have made large boxes with wheels for trees, shrubs, and evergreens on terraces and patios or for decoration at entranceways. Use durable wood—redwood or cypress—as these will remain outdoors all year around. Woods that deteriorate will require treatment with a non-toxic preservative, like Cuprinol, which is not harmful to plants.

Clean and scrub clay and plastic pots—whether for outdoor or indoor use—using warm sudsy water and wiping with a piece of cloth to remove remnants of dirt on the outside. If you do not have shelves to store these and other garden tools and supplies, make shelves so they will be off the floor of the basement or cellar and take up less space.

Take inventory of what supplies you will need for the growing season.

*From late winter onward start to repot house plants, using larger containers. Add organic matter when mixing the soil.*

*Feed house plants, starting in late February when days are longer. Use liquid or dry fertilizer in suggested amounts.*

Do not wait too long as spring has a way of rushing in unexpectedly, and if you are to order through catalogues, items often take several weeks to come.

Before you realize it will be time to move supplies and equipment to their summer headquarters, generally the garage or tool house. So be ready when the first warm days signal the time to prune, apply dormant sprays, plant hardy trees and shrubs when the soil is soft and workable. A tool house can be an attractive addition to the garden, sometimes complete with window boxes of gay geraniums and a weather vane on top. If you need storage space, consider buying a ready-made one, making your own, or engaging a carpenter so you can make it the right size for your needs.

Lastly, though not connected with the outdoors, comes house plant care. Winter is the perfect time to give them the added attention they will need. Plants may require repotting and feeding as lengthening days stimulate new growth—and flowering. Where spray is needed, adhere to directions on packages carefully as severe damage and even death can be inflicted if improper amounts are used.

*Winter is the time to paint garden stakes, window boxes, tubs, trellises, and garden furniture in the basement.*

# Part Three

GETTING READY
FOR SPRING

# 1

## Spring Cleanup

THE FIRST STEP in spring cleanup is the removal of debris and litter collected during the winter. On the first pleasant day when the snow has melted, get to work with the rake, using light short strokes. Bamboo or lightweight metal types with curved tines are best to rake leaves from lawns as they do not uproot grass.

Metal rakes with long tines can be worked among shrubs and perennials where excess leaves have accumulated. Enclosed gardens, shut in by houses, garages, and fences suffer the most as they act as repositories for leaves that are whirled about during gales. Gather leaves from among small shrubs, perennials, and rock garden plants by hand, wearing a pair of snug gloves.

Mild weather induces plants such as biennial canterbury bells, foxgloves, and sweet williams, and perennial delphiniums, columbines, and violas to spurt into growth. Tender perennials (like rosemary and tritoma) stored in a cold-frame for the winter, and annuals started from seed to give them a head start, will begin their growth as soon as days are mild and sunny. If they have wintered in a cold-frame, open it during the day to harden the new, young growth—so it will not be soft and scorch when plants are lifted later and set out in the garden. Be certain to close it at night if there is danger of frost.

You can start seeds of annuals now. An excellent medium to use is sphagnum moss as it is sterile and prevents damping-off disease from destroying small seedlings. Perlite, vermiculite, and terra-lite are other sterile mediums that can be used to store seeds of all kinds, not only annuals. If using soil, be certain it is well drained, and then treat both the soil and the seed with a fungicide, again to stop damping-off disease. Many kinds are available at all nurseries and garden centers, but follow directions carefully. If you do, you will have no failures. Seeds of hardy annuals can be sown in the open ground, and these include California poppies, cleome, cosmos, flowering tobacco, snapdragons, and sweet alyssum.

Sweep away winter's accumulation of sand used to prevent slipping

*Use a watering wand or hose to wash soot and grime from evergreens in early spring, particularly in city gardens.*

*When starting annuals and other seedlings in a cold-frame, open up on warm days so they will harden off.*

*Cold-frame with foxgloves and English daisies opened in early spring so plants will adjust to sun before being set out.*

*Moonflower seedlings started indoors in pots are put outside in warm weather to acclimatize prior to planting in ground.*

*In early spring clean, tidy up, bring out supplies, and organize outdoor work area to ready it for summer.*

*There are always leaves to pick up in early spring, no matter how well you cleaned in fall.*

during ice and snow. An ordinary broom will suffice for walks and steps, but for sidewalks and driveways you will need a stiff push broom. After you sweep these areas free of sand, wash them down with a strong force of the hose to make them sparkling clean.

City gardeners have a chore that those in the country do not—washing plants, particularly evergreens, with the hose to help get rid of the accumulation of soot and grime. Not only does the residue of our increasingly polluted air make boxwoods, rhododendrons, and yews look black and grimy, but this thick coating prevents them from breathing normally. Spring rains do help, but you will get better results with a stiff spray of the hose.

Part of spring cleanup is getting the storage area ready for use. Whether tools and supplies were stored in the basement, cellar, tool house, shed, or attic, they will need organizing to get ready for the season's use. Place the hose where it will be handy, the lawn mower where it will stay for the season, the pruning shears where they can be located when needed, sprays where they will be safe and in a place that is not too hot. If you have a tool house or potting shed, place equipment and supplies in their permanent positions. Bring out pots and other containers, fill covered cans with soil, peat moss, perlite, sand, and whatever else you want to pot plants for outdoor—and indoor—use. Furniture can be brought out to the terrace or porch, and if cleaned and covered during the winter, a light dusting with a cloth will suffice. Just get ready, and the sooner the better. You'll find that your gardening will be that much easier and more pleasurable.

# 2

## Take Off Winter Covers
## and Untie Plants

WHEN SHOULD WINTER protection covers be removed from plants and statues? One might think the disappearance of snow is a sure sign, but do not be too hasty. Plants protected with laths, boards, or burlap receive enough light and air to survive as they did during the winter. Early spring is always unpredictable, so just go slowly. The chief danger is an unexpected snowstorm that might cause breakage. Other than that, hardy trees and shrubs of all kinds can withstand sun and air and whatever early spring weather brings.

Covers made of laths and boards fall into two categories: those that have been nailed and must be taken apart, and those that are snug-fitting units. The first usually need a hammer or an ax to separate, while the others are simply disconnected. Save the sections, as they can be used again and again, especially if they have been painted or stained to help preserve the wood. Dust with a moist cloth or wash down thoroughly with the hose, allowing to dry in the sun before storing for the summer. If necessary give them a coat of paint before using again in the fall. When removing, be careful not to break any of the branches of the plants.

Involved, too, is burlap, whether used in pieces nailed to stakes along the sides of rhododendrons or wrapped around tender blue hydrangeas or boxwoods and secured to a stake. It can be dried, rolled neatly, tied, and stored for reuse next year.

Snow fences can easily be taken away, washed with the hose, allowed to dry, rolled, and tied before storing for the summer and fall. Snow fences are strong, durable, and attractive, so take good care of them as they are a great aid in winter protection of plants. Wire fencing of many kinds including chicken wire, recommended to guard a low formal hedge against breakage, simply needs to be unfastened from its stakes, rolled, tied with rope or strong string, and stored wherever you have space. It will last and be serviceable "forever." Where snowplows shove snow against these wire-protected hedges or where children play in the area, it

*A quick way to secure deciduous shrubs, as an azalea, is
to insert a wooden stake and tie its branches with twine.*

is better to use metal rods rather than wooden stakes which break easily.
The rods will serve you for more years than you can count.

More gardeners are realizing the importance of covering statues,
figures, pools, fountains, and other costly and important accessories.
Though normally meant to stay in the garden all year around, protecting
them in winter will prolong their life. The best way to cover statues,
figures, and other ornaments is by placing specially built wooden frames
over them. They can be painted the color of the house, or better still a
dark green or black to make them less conspicuous. Marble and
concrete statues and figures are usually first wrapped with large sheets
of plastic to keep out moisture.

After removing the wooden frames from the statues, take the plastic
off, dry if wet or moist, roll or fold, and store in a dry place until next
fall. As with laths and wooden structures, do not be too hasty. Spring
storms may bring snow and a coating of ice, which can be quite damaging and often irreparable.

*Statue of a Roman matron was wrapped with plastic, covered*
*with a wooden frame, with balsam fir trees on the outside.*

Before the frames are put away, be sure they are strong and sturdy,
firm where joined, and if nails or screws are loose, tighten with a hammer
or screw driver. Make any repairs right away rather than in late fall
when you may want to install them quickly, especially if weather sud-
denly turns cold.

If some plants have grown too large for their props, prune to control
their size. If you want them larger, you may need new structures, and
spring and summer are good times to have new ones made.

Many gardeners protect their plants against winter breakage by tying
them with rope, heavy string, and often strong wire. The method is simple, quick, and effective, especially on large shrubs that have thick
enough branches to stand up against the weight of snow and ice. The
plants can be tied to one or more stakes—usually three or four around
each specimen. Small plants, ones newly planted, are more safely
steadied by coverings of laths, pieces of boards, or baskets.

When should your plants be untied? Certainly, for one, the snow should have melted, and the grass ought to have areas of green. You should watch for bud breaking, which means the shrub is ready to flower or burst into leaf. Those plants that break buds early need to be freed soonest.

During winter get the few tools you will need ready, that is, make certain pruning shears, strong scissors, wire cutters, and knives are well-sharpened, so you can do the job quickly without the frustration that accompanies tools that do not cut or work properly.

As you free plants try to salvage as much of the string, rope, or other

*A garden figure can be covered with plastic, then shielded from snow and ice with a pyramid-shaped wooden frame.*

Garden statues at Essex Institute in Salem, Massachusetts, protected with wooden structures that can be used again.

In summer, revealed under one of the frames, is a graceful garden figure amid the greenery of Boston ivy and hostas.

material as possible. If shrubs are tied and knotted at several places, do not try, but simply cut in order not to break any of the branches. If long pieces of rope or other materials are in good condition, roll neatly, secure, and store for reuse the next fall.

As you work keep a basket or carton by your side to toss in the small pieces of rope. You can do some pruning at the same time, another reason tools and pruning shears should be sharp. Cut and remove branches that are obviously dead or in weakened condition or any that may be broken. It is a labor- and time-saving device, untying and pruning at the same time. If you're not certain whether branches are alive or dead, leave them alone and do the pruning after buds burst when you will know immediately which are dead and which are not.

If stakes have been used, work on a day when the soil is not frozen but is soft and thawed so the stakes can be pulled up easily. Wash and clean them with a stiff brush, wipe with a piece of cloth, and place in the sun for a few hours to dry before storing. If tied in bunches and placed upright or along the wall of the basement, cellar, or garage, they will take little space.

You may plan to use these stakes for other tall garden plants, as cimicifugas, delphiniums, hollyhocks, sunflowers, and tomatoes. Whether used again or stored, it is advisable to paint wooden ones before next use.

*The time to take away winter shields, as burlap around rhododendrons, is when snow melts and grass is green.*

# 3

## Remove Winter Mulches

TIMING IS IMPORTANT in the removal of winter mulches and winter blankets. On the one hand you want to be sure the danger of frost has passed. But keeping mulches on too long can result in soft premature growth coming through the mulch. Even worse, the mulch, because of its heaviness, will smother the plant.

Winter blankets are generally removed entirely. When a heavy layer of marsh hay or straw is placed around hybrid tea roses, it is all taken away. When beds or plantings of Dutch bulbs are covered with used or unsold Christmas trees, the latter are all picked up and discarded. In many cases the lighter winter mulches are thinned and only partially removed.

How do you determine the proper timing? If you've lived in an area long enough, you get to know the prevailing climate quite well. But if you have recently moved, you will find that gardening in one part of the country is drastically different from another. Don't hesitate to watch or ask gardening neighbors more familiar with your locale. Consult them and, better still, consult state and county experiment stations by phone or letter.

When you do proceed, the first step in uncovering winter-protected plants is to loosen the mulches and let in air and sun. While weather remains cold there is little cause for alarm, but as days become warmer, growth may start and if the mulch is particularly moist, smothering may follow. If possible, remove mulches on a cloudy day. If not taken off in time and growth has started, lanky shoots may appear above the tops of the mulches.

Areas that need first attention are those along the sunny sides of the house or garage, along fences, walls, ledges and rock outcroppings where you grow alpines and herbs. If growth has already started, be gentle when loosening or removing the mulches—the soft yellow shoots can break easily if they are several inches tall.

*In early spring winter blankets, as wood chips around this lilac, can be loosened, spread out, and left for the season.*

If the weatherman announces a sudden drop to freezing or below, the already-loosened mulches are easily replaced. Then as the weather warms up, remove the mulches entirely from the roses, bulbs, perennials, rock plants, herbs, and other plants, but still leave on the ground around and near the plants. The reason? To replace in the event of a frost threat. It is amazing how late frosts can come, even after trees have come into full leaf. Not too many years ago a severe one occurred on May 30 in the Boston area.

The most useful tool for loosening mulches and placing them to one side is the spading fork—which will also remove mulches entirely when the time comes. Another good tool is the metal long-tined rake—large or small, depending on the width of borders and spacing of plants. A long-handled weeder can also do the job. A long stick, as the end of an old broom or a dahlia stake, is functional. Or you can do some of the close work by hand, wearing snug-fitting strong gloves. Thick layers that are winter blankets—peat moss, shredded bark, wood chips, buckwheat hulls, or other material—should be loosened with a tool.

*Light, loose, and airy marsh hay provides a young rhodo-dendron with protection from winter's cold, wind, and sun.*

*Removing marsh hay placed around a hybrid tea rose in the early spring when it is warm and danger of injury is over.*

What do you do with the removed mulches? Some kinds can only be thrown away. Others, like chopped up evergreens, can be relegated to the compost pile. Both straw and marsh hay can be stored in cartons or large plastic bags, placed in the basement, cellar, garage, or shed for the summer to be used again in the fall. As a rule they can be spread around garden flowers but are useful around vegetables and small fruits as blueberries, raspberries, strawberries, and other brambles.

You can lessen the thickness of fine mulches like peat moss, shredded bark, or wood chips and leave them in place as regular summer mulch. You will save the effort of applying mulch in the spring and is recommended if you want to have a good garden. What you remove can be spread around other plants in the garden or stored to use again the following fall.

*The right time to take away winter mulches or blankets is always tricky, but you can watch knowledgeable neighbors.*

# 4

## Pest and Weed Control

SPRAYING WITH CHEMICALS is difficult business. Kinds that have proven useful when first introduced can turn out to have long-range detrimental effects, as in the case of DDT. Nevertheless, chemical sprays of many kinds have been around for a long time, and they are here to stay. When using them we must proceed with caution, use each type carefully, and follow directions word for word. Only then will beneficial results be possible.

Certain basic precautionary measures should be adhered to when using garden sprays. If you are going to dust or spray, do so in the early morning. The air is more apt to be still and air temperatures are cooler. Adopt an integrated pest-control program by following good cultural practices, sanitation, crop rotation, mechanical controls, and biological aids (as planting nasturtiums to repel Mexican bean and cucumber beetles) to reduce the need for pesticide use.

Take care to avoid contact with the skin, and wear plastic or rubber gloves. Do not smoke, eat, or drink when spraying. Check sprayers and other equipment carefully before using to make certain there no leaks, and do your mixing outdoors, never indoors—and then only in the garage or basement in winter for house plants. Close bottles and other packages tightly after using, and always keep pesticides in their original containers. Place under lock and key where necessary, more so where there are children in the family. Most important of all, never use more than the amount specified on the containers.

For the home gardener, early spring is the time for dormant spraying, the kinds applied to a great variety of plants when they are still "asleep," before they begin to awaken. Dormant sprays have many advantages. One, they are applied when most plants are leafless and easily seen, at a time when the full pressure of spring has not begun. Another is that they control some insects and some diseases in the egg and spore stage, before they have a chance to cause any damage. All evergreens are somewhat sensitive to oil, especially Douglas fir and blue spruce.

*Dormant sprays can be applied to trees and shrubs in early spring, as lime-sulphur to control infestations of aphids.*

One of the best dormant sprays is lime-sulphur, applied in the early spring to woody plants of many kinds before leaf buds and flowers break, about the time pussy willow buds start to display their silver. Lime-sulphur will check aphids, which appear during the growing season; scale on euonymus, lilacs, and other plants; and red spider mites, common on evergreens. It is also effective on fruit trees, roses, and many other kinds of woody plants. Apply when temperature is over 40° F., up to a high of 65° F. and likely to stay well above freezing for a period of forty-eight hours. One caution about lime-sulphur: keep away from painted and concrete surfaces, like houses and fences, as it discolors.

An oil-emulsion spray, sold under various trade names, as Volck and Scalecide, also known as miscible oil, is excellent for scale on euonymus. It will also control the eggs of mites and aphids on needle evergreens,

*Scale, the most common pest on evergreen euonymus, should
be sprayed with oil in early spring, following directions.*

destroying them before they start their damage. Like lime-sulphur, it
should be used when the temperatures are above 40° F. No matter what,
hardly enough emphasis can be placed on using it as directed.

Neither lime-sulphur nor oil emulsion can be used on thin-barked
trees, as they will cause injury. These include beeches, Douglas fir, false
cypresses, hemlocks, hickories, larches, magnolias, sugar, Japanese, and
other maples, walnuts, and yews.

A miscible oil can be applied to apple, pear, and other fruit trees in
the very early spring before buds show any green, applying at the rates
listed on the labels and always giving a thorough covering. On fruits,
spraying is essential to insure insect and disease-free fruits. When in
doubt about what to use—and when—get in touch with county extension
services or agricultural experiment stations which distribute literature on
how to spray fruit and ornamental trees and shrubs.

Weeds begin their growth in early spring, and this is another area that requires knowledge and extra patience. So many varieties of weed killers are available at nurseries and garden centers it is difficult for the novice to know which is best. When in doubt read the label and do not hesitate to ask either well-informed clerks or to consult with experts at government experiment centers. Preliminary caution can save the life of many a plant.

Weed killers are known as herbicides. They vary widely in their chemical compositions and toxic action, so must be applied with the same reluctance as dormant sprays on the trunks and branches of woody trees and shrubs. Some are selective; that is, they will kill only certain plants without injuring others. Some are non-selective—they kill all plants, and must be used more carefully and with extreme caution.

*Biological control methods are becoming popular, as nasturtiums with squash to repel Mexican and cucumber beetles.*

One of the safest pre-emergence herbicides is Dacthal G-5 which can be used in flower borders to control crab grass and other annual grasses and certain broad-leaved weeds on mineral soils, among them wild mustard and ragweed. Though it does not need to be cultivated into the soil, avoid disturbing after it has been applied. It is toxic to some garden plants, as ajuga, carnations, geum, pansies, phlox, and sweet williams. Therefore, use with extreme caution.

Eptam (EPTC) is another safe and highly recommended herbicide. If applied at the beginning of the season, it will stop most weeds in established annual and perennial borders before they start. It is also safe to use on established plantings of shrubs, roses, and ground covers, where weeds have an insidious way of creeping in. First remove existing weeds, and then cultivate the soil, shaking the granules of Eptam evenly over the soil. Cultivate into the soil to a depth of two or three inches, and water well. Eptam will not control weeds that are already growing.

Betasan (Bensulide) is one of the many pre-emergence crab-grass killers. It is effective only on established lawns. It should *not* be used on lawn areas to be seeded or those that have recently been seeded. Tupersan (Siduron) will prevent crab grass without affecting other lawn grasses.

In the non-selective group, if you want to get rid of certain annual and perennial grasses, use Dowpon (Dalapon), which must be applied after weeds or other undesirable plants have appeared. It is excellent for tough grasses, as Bermuda grass, Johnson grass, foxtail, and quack grass. Generally, because it sterilizes soil for a month, you cannot reseed immediately.

The most familiar selective herbicide to control broad-leaved weeds in lawns is 2,4-D. It will kill dandelions, plantains, mustards, and other broad-leaved weeds. Care must be taken that it does not drift on other nearby plants.

Another well-known herbicide is Weed-B-Gon (2,4-D, Banvel D), which will destroy many kinds of broad-leaved weeds on lawns. Weedone (Amitrole) is your answer to eliminating poison ivy or poison oak. Since it is highly toxic to lawns and other plants, it must be used with extra care.

# 5

## Repair Winter Damage

WINTER TAKES ITS TOLL on both the living and non-living parts of your garden, no matter what precautions you take. The plants that undergo the greatest damage are the trees, shrubs, and vines even if they have had some protection. Perennials and bulbs do not escape; some die from cold or poor drainage; others, like chrysanthemums, may be heaved out of the ground by thawing and refreezing.

Catastrophe can hit trees and shrubs, primarily large specimens that are impossible to cover or protect in other ways. Evergreens take the greatest beating because in leaf they bear the brunt of snow more than deciduous trees, whose naked branches allow the snow to glide through.

To repair trees, shrubs, and vines, cut off dead and damaged wood. If you cannot tell which branches are dead, wait until first buds begin to break. Where branches are broken make clean cuts to the nearest crotch with sharp pruning shears or a saw and cover with tree-wound paint. Do not leave stubs, but cut the branches completely so natural callouses can form to heal cuts more quickly and effectively. To avoid bark stripping downward, cut the heavy branches in parts, leaving short stubs; then remove the stubs and apply the tree-wound paint.

Branches may split with the weight of snow or the strength of wind. These can often be saved if the two sections are first tied into position with rope and the wounded portions covered with grafting wax or tree-wound paint to keep out moisture. Wrap the split branch completely in tree wrap and leave this way for two years before removing. If the weight of any of the split branches is too heavy, cut off some of the top to lighten it. In spring much new growth will appear to fill in. No further attention will be needed during the course of the two years, except to make certain the rope is not cutting into the bark.

If bark from a tree or shrub was stripped by snow or ice, remove ragged edges with a sharp knife, shaping the wound so it is narrow, with a sharp V point at the downward end. Paint the edges and entire wound

*Japanese tree lilac in author's garden, shown in color on the jacket, was broken severely in a later snowstorm and took years to recover after pruned, fed, and shaped.*

with shellac to make it moisture proof, and when dry cover with tree-wound paint or with dark-colored oil-based paint.

Bark splitting, or sunscald, is another kind of winter damage more common on newly planted trees, those with thin barks, or any not fully hardy. The damage occurs mostly on the sunny side, where bark expands with the warmth of the sun, then contracts when the thermometer drops at night. With a sharp knife, cut back to healthy wood, making neat edges, then sealing with tree-wound paint. In time callous tissue will cover the exposed wood and heal the splitting. To prevent sunscald, trunks of trees likely to be affected can be covered in early fall with tree wrap, working it spirally from the base upward.

Damage caused to bark by automobiles or snowplows is more severe and the wounds larger and wider. To repair, cut edges of bark with a sharp knife, trimming in a downward eclipse position so rain will wash downward, smoothing the wood if the gouge is deep. Then apply the usual healing and protective paint.

*This is how crab apple in author's garden, in color on the cover, looked after a blizzard smashed and broke it badly.*

*The same crab apple being pruned in May, before flowering, with a sharp saw to remove broken branches and to shape.*

*Unless braced, tall, slender arborvitae will bend over with the weight of snow. They rarely recover completely.*

Evergreens often succumb to windburning, the result of sun and wind action on leaves that are giving off moisture they are unable to replace before the ground is frozen. Dead branches and leaves result, evidenced in late spring or early summer. When this happens, simply cut off the branch. If plants have been severely mauled, it is advisable to strengthen them by feeding.

Sometimes plants are located where drainage is poor. If possible, remove plants that do not grow well in moist locations to another spot in the garden, replacing them with those that will. If they cannot be moved, lift smaller plants and add sand, peat moss, or perlite to the soil to lighten it and improve drainage.

Damage can occur to terraces, patios, and walks, whether brick, bluestone, or concrete. You may be handy and able to repair them yourself. If not, engage a qualified workman. Paths, walls, and steps are permanent features that may be damaged by ice, rain, and the general passage of time. Fences, trellises, and arbors, too, should not be overlooked. Give them attention and repair work required as soon as you notice the damage—before it spreads, becomes dangerous, or unsightly.

# 6

## Time to Paint

EARLY SPRING, when weather is pleasant, is the time to paint garden accessories, fences, trellises, arbors, window boxes, planters, and other containers—wooden as well as metal—and terrace and porch furniture.

Do it before leaves appear, and be sure all wood has dried out from winter freezing and rain. With yearly painting, no scraping is generally required. If paint has begun to peel, scrape and apply two new coats of paint. Use high-quality outdoor paint—consult your local paint dealer for the best type—and use good, firm brushes, preferably made of hair. Plastic brushes do not give as good a finish and do not last as long—tend to streak.

It is also imperative to paint early where plants, like vines on trellises and arbors, are involved—before growth starts. Take care not to get any paint on stems, as it stays for years and is unattractive.

Vines, unlike empty window boxes, present the greatest problem. If non-twiners, like climbing roses, they can be loosened entirely and allowed to rest on the ground. Then you can paint without the interference of stems. Small vines, like clematis, can also be unfastened, but do it early, as growth appears soon on clematis and is very fragile. The same applies to climbing roses and grapes.

Vigorous twiners, like bittersweet and wisteria on an arbor, present considerable difficulty. Actually, they should offer hardly any hindrance at all if you train twining vines properly when young, just after planting. Instead of allowing them to twine on their permanent supports, permit several stems to climb on string or rope. When the stems become thick and heavy enough, they can be attached to the trellis with heavy twine or rope—as you treat climbing roses. Then when painting, some of the tangled growth can be trimmed, but the main stems can be unfastened and permitted to fall on the ground. If your arbor or trellis needs to be replaced, transferring the vines will not be difficult.

Wooden fences without vines are easy to paint, though tedious. Much

*When painting window boxes and other garden features, choose a warm sunny day when wood is dry. Apply two coats if needed.*

in use are low wooden fences that can be lifted, folded in sections, and stored for the winter. On the whole they work quite well, acting as an obstruction to dogs and cats.

To cut down on maintenance, fences, furniture, sun decks, and other features can be stained. Better still are woods such as cypress and redwood which are not painted or stained but allowed to weather, taking on a soft gray tone that harmonizes with all colors. Other woods are treated with a preservative, like Cuprinol, that is non-toxic to plants. This is important and frequently overlooked, often with fence posts inserted into the ground, where rot and decay occur much faster than the upper portions in the sun and air.

When selecting colors for window boxes, keep in mind the hues of the flowers you plan to grow in them. Dark blossoms, as ageratum, blue lobelia, and browallia, do not show up against dark surfaces. The same applies to light-colored blossoms, as white geraniums and petunias in white window boxes attached to a white house. In such an instance, there would be hardly any contrast at all, except for foliage. All this is a matter of taste, but what is important is that you paint whatever needs it as early in the spring as possible before growth starts and the pressure of spring gardening makes its heavy demands.

# 7

## Early Spring Feeding and Mulching

PLANTS MUST BE fertilized if they are to grow properly. Also essential for growth are mulches, and the two go hand-in-hand. Both can be applied at the same time—fertilizers first followed by mulches—either in late fall or early spring. Balanced chemical foods, which stimulate quick, fast growth, are best applied in the spring or during periods of active development and flowering.

Feed your plants before buds break into leaf and flower, just as warm weather brings on the first flush of growth. All kinds of plants can be fed in the early spring, late spring, or early summer—trees, shrubs, perennials, bulbs, herbs, annuals, and vegetables. The general rule is to avoid feeding trees, shrubs, vines, and other woody plants after the middle of summer (mid-July in the North), as it stimulates late season growth, and results in much winterkilling of wood that has insufficient time to harden before cold weather.

Each kind of plant has its own fertilizer requirements. Lawns like a food with high nitrogen to promote leafy growth. Peonies need phosphoric acid to encourage blooming. It is a good policy to keep several kinds of fertilizers on hand and vary their uses, following directions for amounts, whether dealing with trees, shrubs, perennials, or annuals. Do not give too much, especially chemical kinds, as they can "burn." Fertilizers must also be used on moist soils, and watering should be followed. So read instructions with care—this cannot be stressed strongly enough.

Fertilizers can be applied in varying ways and with different types of tools. Trees and large shrubs, with their deep root systems, will need feeding with a crowbar or a root feeder. Depth depends on the size of the plants, though it is usually a foot to a foot and a half. Fertilizer for perennials, whose roots are close to the surface, can be scattered with a trowel or by hand, usually at the rate of three to four pounds per one hundred square feet in the case of a 5-10-5 or 7-8-7 formula. Most important is to feed regularly at least once a year, best in early spring so plants

*To feed azaleas and other shrubs and trees in early spring,
make holes about a foot deep with a crowbar.*

*Then place a trowelful of fertilizer in each hole, with
soil on top. Water deeply so food will start activating.*

will benefit fully from the nutrients supplied them.

Do not overlook plants in containers such as planters, boxes, and urns. Fed each spring, they can remain in the same containers for several years. In the case of window boxes, replenish with soil well-supplied with humus and fertilizer, or scatter food and scratch in before planting time. Don't forget to repot and feed house plants, though not an actual part of the outdoor garden. Many will be taken outdoors for the summer and should be fertilized in spring when they begin to grow as a result of increased sunlight and day length.

Fertilizers are either organic or inorganic. Old manure, dehydrated manure (processed), dried blood, tankage, bone meal, and cottonseed meal are organic. Since these foods are slow acting, and therefore safe, they can be applied in the fall or early winter. Inorganics act quickly, giving fast results, and are best used in the early spring. They include nitrate of soda, ammonium sulphate, cyanamid, and urea. Both types can be given most plants, and the ideal combination consists of some of both —the organic because it supplies humus, the inorganic since it responds quickly. There are some gardeners, however, who believe in natural gardening and use only organic fertilizers.

In the inorganic group some of the most common are 5-10-10, recommended for all kinds of plants; 10-6-4, often sold for lawns because of its high nitrogen content; and 12-12-12, a general purpose food for all plants, flowering and foliage. It does not matter which balanced fertilizer you select, provided it is given in the right amounts at the right time. To be on the safe side, apply less and feed more often. The first numeral in a fertilizer combination, as in 5-10-5, represents the amount of nitrogen, indicated by the letter N. The second is for phosphorous or phosphoric acid, symbolized by P. The third, also P, is for the percentage of potash or potassium.

Nitrogen, the first, is for leaf and stem growth, recommended for leafy ornamentals as coleus and ferns, grass, and leafy vegetables like lettuce. Because it acts quickly, is absorbed the fastest, and must be replenished most often, it is best given in the spring. Soils are usually lowest in nitrogen in the spring, and a summer of heavy rains will leach it from the soil. It also gives plants a healthy dark green coloring.

Phosphorous or phosphoric acid releases quickly and is soluble. Since it does not move or travel in the soil quickly it must be worked in deeply, near the roots where it can be effective. It encourages the production of flowers, fruits, and seeds on such plants as roses, dogwoods, and tomatoes. Hastening flowering and maturity, it also promotes hardiness. Sources for phosphorous include bone meal, superphosphate, rock phosphate, and basic slug. Superphosphate or bone meal are often applied to plants, as dogwood and wisterias, which often fail to flower.

Potash, or potassium, needs periodic replenishing, though its level

*Root feeder with fertilizer cartridge and water that pours through hose is a good way to feed trees, shrubs, and other plants as it places food deep in ground, at feeding roots.*

tends to remain constant in the soil from year to year. Its purpose is to stimulate sturdy root growth in all plants, particularly those with fleshy roots like bulbs, iris, and peonies, and root-crop vegetables—potatoes, carrots, and beets. It also helps to increase the size, flavor, and vigor of some fruits and vegetables, along with increasing resistance to certain diseases in plants. Sources of potash include muriate of potash, potassium chloride, potassium sulphate, and wood ashes.

In addition to these big three, there are so-called trace elements that supply different nutrients. Yellowing or discolored foliage often indicates a lack of trace elements, which include boron, zinc, magnesium, manganese, copper, sulphur, calcium, and molybdenum. Correct amounts where needed aid in improving imbalances, but must be used carefully, as most soils possess sufficient amounts. Follow directions for proportions as overdoses can be harmful.

Along with feeding in early spring, mulches should be applied. Mulches are proving invaluable in the garden, retaining moisture in the

*One of the most important springtime chores is to spread an organic mulch in tree, shrub, and flower borders. Here wood chips are being spread around iris. Mulches keep soil moist.*

soil, helping prevent excessive weed growth (not entirely), leveling off temperatures so that soils stay cooler, adding humus to soils in the case of organic mulches, eliminating cultivating, and improving overall appearance.

The successful gardener is definitely the one who mulches. Two kinds are used: organic, as peat moss, buckwheat hulls, and marsh hay; and inorganic, as stones, pebbles, and plastic film. The value of the organic mulch is that it decomposes and returns to the soil, improving its texture and friability. Finer kinds, as peat moss or ground corncobs, are recommended for flower and rose beds since they are more refined. Coarser organics, as marsh hay and wood chips, can be spread around trees, shrubs, and in the vegetable garden.

The usual depth for a mulch is two to three inches, spread evenly but not too close to the crown of plants or they will stay too wet and soft. Then insects and disease organisms will tend to infect barks and stems because of lack of sunlight.

Apply the mulch after snow has disappeared, when soil has softened, when visible signs of spring (like the bursting of buds on trees and shrubs) are on their way. There is no need to do it before weeds begin heavy growth. If weeds are evident, first either pull them or use a weed killer. Applied early enough, weed growth will be at a minimum, as many weed seeds do not have the strength to push through a layer that is two or three inches thick. If a mulch is a light scattering, barely enough to cover the soil's surface, do not expect much in the way of weed control or effectiveness.

Organic mulches are the most popular, led by peat moss (dried and pressed sphagnum moss), excellent for roses, perennials, annuals, and bulbs. It should be wet before applying. Its one great disadvantage is that it does not absorb water easily when dry, so try to keep it constantly moist. Peat may be either sedge or reed, dark in coloring, and must be used three or more inches thick to thwart weed growth.

*Hardy container plants, as this Japanese tree maple, can be removed from their clay pots, which are breakable, and dug in ground for the winter. First wrap ball of soil with burlap.*

*Replacing Japanese red maple in its clay pot after dug from the
ground in spring. After burlap is removed, some roots are cut.*

*Soil is removed from the top of the ball of earth and new mix-
ture, fortified with fertilizer and organic matter, is applied.*

*The next step is to prune, since the tree has been in the same pot for several years. This eliminates some of the top the roots need to support and gives the tree character, making it look like bonsai.*

Leafmold, flaky and dark, is another excellent refined organic mulch, increasingly difficult to obtain, and recommended for ferns and wild flowers as well as all kinds of annual and perennial flowering plants in borders. Like peat moss and peat, it is dug into the soil at planting time. Buckwheat hulls are also hard to find. They are light and airy so water penetrates them easily, but they tend to wash away in heavy downpours. Peanut hulls, cranberry branches, cottonseed hulls or meal with an acid reaction are recommended for azaleas, camellias, gardenias, rhododendrons, and other acid-loving plants.

Sawdust is another good mulch for flower borders because it is fine, especially if partly decayed, when it is deeper in color. High-nitrogen fertilizer, absorbed in the decomposition process, should be applied with

*The same Japanese tree maple, ten years old, as it looked with fresh growth on May 14. Little pruning may be needed later, but not much.*

sawdust, coarser wood chips, shredded bark, and tree shavings. One pound of nitrate of soda or sulfate of ammonia suffices for a bushel of any of these mulches.

For trees and shrubs—mostly in naturalistic plantings—and for vegetables, rely on clean, airy, disease-free marsh hay, straw, or bean straw if obtainable. All are excellent for fruit trees and can be used as winter blankets, removed in the early spring, stored for the summer, and used again the following season.

*Feeding shallow-rooted plants (perennials, bulbs, rock plants and herbs) in early spring can be done by scattering mixed fertilizer by hand. Be certain to distribute evenly, and to water soil thoroughly.*

Ground corncobs are attractive, retain moisture, and control weeds, suiting them to flower borders or beds. Light in color and of good texture, they should be used in combination with a fertilizer. Cocoa bean hulls have fertilizer value but should not be applied too thickly. Root surface may be injured if spread too deep, particularly around azaleas and rhododendrons. Two inches is enough.

Seaweed can be gathered along the coast to use as mulch. Though not attractive, it is valued for its nutrients and is best dug into the soil as it decays slowly. Tobacco stems and coffee grounds are good mulches, as are grass clippings if not put on too heavily (though weeds may tend to develop). If you can obtain old manure well decomposed so it will not burn, consider yourself lucky. Compost also has many merits as a soil conditioner and mulch.

There's nothing new about using several layers of papers laid between rows on seed beds to keep weeds in check, or between rows of vegetables, but somehow they seem to have been forgotten. Redwood chips are coarse, best confined to trees and shrubs but not around small flowers because they are too large. They control weeds excellently and decompose slowly, lasting a long time. When new their coloring is orange-brown, not harmonious with colors of some flowers, but with time turn brown. Among organic mulches do not neglect pine needles. They are fine, do not smother small plants, look natural, and are pungent when hot sun strikes them. Use around acid-loving plants and native wild flowers.

Inorganic mulches vary in their uses and purposes and do not decompose, making them long lasting, an advantage over organic. Their primary disadvantage is that they can become covered with leaves and other debris, so cleaning them is a necessary—and not often easy—chore.

Vermiculite, perlite, and terra-lite can be spread around flowers, both perennials and annuals, and plants in containers. Used in large quantities, they tend to be expensive but perform well when it comes to controlling moisture and weeds. All are attractive and refined. Crushed stones and pebbles are also inorganic and add an architectural quality wherever placed. However, they must be cleaned of falling leaves and flower petals in the fall and early spring, and this task can be an enormous one.

Black polyethylene is ideal in the vegetable garden but not for the flower garden. Spread between rows, weeds are held in check, moisture is retained, and cultivating is eliminated, but make slits so water and air can pass through. Black polyethylene absorbs the heat of the sun, which means vegetables start to produce sooner. Aluminum foil and glass wool, also inorganic, are coming more and more into use, mostly for vegetable gardens and plantings of small fruits, as blueberries and raspberries. Volcanic rock, still little known, may be dark gray or red in coloring and is available in pebble size. Handsome yet durable it is recommended for container gardening on balconies and rooftops because of its light weight, something to consider when gardening above ground.

# 8

## Prune in the Early Spring

ONE OF THE MOST important early spring chores is proper pruning of trees and shrubs. Though much pruning can be done in late fall or winter, plants not reliably hardy—such as butterfly bush, caryopteris, rose of sharon, roses of many kinds, and vitex—should only be pruned in early spring since winter will do much killing. If you have not pruned your hardy plants in fall or winter, spring weather is ideal—warm and safe for all kinds of plants.

Pruning serves many purposes. First, it restrains plants by checking growth. Second, pruning improves appearance. Of all aspects of gardening it, like landscape design, is an art. The more you study pruning techniques and principles, the more you practice them, the better able you will be to make plants look their best. And third, pruning increases vigor, letting in more air and sunlight so flowering and growth are better.

Early spring, before growth starts, is an ideal time to prune deciduous and evergreen trees, shrubs, and vines, especially in colder regions where you have to wait for snow to melt. Prune early and you will have more flexibility than when the rush of spring growth begins, seemingly overnight. If weather remains unseasonably cool, growth is all the more spontaneous when warm, sunny days finally arrive.

Evergreens especially require very early pruning. Unlike deciduous trees and shrubs, evergreens are slower growing and are not as apt to send forth new shoots from the base. Early pruning stimulates the development of latent buds needed to fill gaps left by pruning. Avoid pruning in midsummer or winter as holes remain until new growth develops.

With deciduous trees and shrubs it is easier to see branch structures without interference from leaves and to detect dead or broken branches. To determine if wood is dead, first look at the color. It may be lighter than the live branches. Dead wood breaks easily if pulled by the hand and is easier to remove with a saw than live. If you are uncertain, remove some of the bark, and if there is no green coloring, the wood is dead or dying.

*Overgrown foundation planting with evergreens and azaleas, sheared since planting ten years ago before pruned in spring.*

*Same foundation planting after plants were pruned by hand in early spring, before growth started, with cuttings on ground.*

*Again the same foundation planting showing new growth
by the next fall. Plants were regularly fed and watered.*

Evergreens, which have fixed growing periods, do not fill in from pruning as readily as deciduous trees. Because of this it is important to give them an annual pruning in early spring, which stimulates latent buds and gives the fill-in process a start.

Overgrown trees should be pruned if their low dense branches are cutting off sunlight needed for the grass and flowering plants below them.

Though there is no one correct way to prune, certain techniques give better results. Make certain tools are clean and sharp. If not, they will tear and pull bark and make the task more difficult for you. For the average home gardener, pruning shears, loppers, pole pruners, and several kinds of saws—each performing a different task—suffice for just about all needs. To keep pruning and clipping tools sterile and prevent the spread of diseases from one plant to another, get in the habit of dipping the cutting parts in alcohol before proceeding to the next plant.

Because of the liability risk, engage arborists when it comes to pruning large trees. Adopt the policy of pruning only as far as you can reach with the tallest ladder you have, then leave the rest to an expert.

A basic rule is to cut branches back to a bud, branch, or trunk of the tree or shrub. Do not leave stubs. They are unattractive and may not

Suckers at the base of trees need to be removed. They are common on crab apple as shown on this young lawn specimen.

Cutting suckers with pruning shears from base of the crab apple. Keep removing them, as they recur all season long.

*Sheared, rounded yews along foundation of a garage before pruned to open up and allow new growth to develop naturally.*

*Yews in same foundation planting along garage after pruned by hand with pruning shears on May 11. Cuttings are at base.*

*Same yews photographed on November 18, showing new graceful shoots. Some new shoots were as much as twenty inches long.*

heal, leaving openings for disease and pest invasions. Make all cuts flush with the trunk or branch. Seal them with tree-wound paint applied with an aerosol can on small cuts or with a brush dipped in a can for larger ones. Covering cuts prevents the invasion of infections and moisture. Brushes should be cleaned in paint thinner or gasoline, then washed thoroughly in hot water and soap and allowed to dry before putting away.

To correct the structure of your plants, first study the natural growth habit of each and work with it rather than against it. Above all, do not shear or clip unless dealing with a formal specimen, as a boxwood in the center of a rose garden, or a formal hedge. If weak V-shaped crotches are present on trees, remove one of the branches or brace it. Trees to avoid pruning in the early spring because they bleed include beeches, birches, maples, and walnuts. They are better pruned in late summer or early fall.

Pruning has a rejuvenating effect on shrubs. Overgrown specimens, as often found in gardens of neglected houses one buys, can be either cut back to the ground or "opened up" by removing some of the oldest branches directly to the ground, a practice recommended yearly to keep

*Author's garden pool, with rhododendron, euonymus, yews, roses, juniper, and English ivy before pruned on April 24.*

*The same pool after it was pruned severely to keep plants in control. Mixed fertilizer was applied and then watered.*

*Pool as it appeared on June 12, showing new, natural growth and rhododendron in bloom. The pruning is done each spring.*

shrubs vigorous, natural, and free flowering. Best pruned this way are forsythias, Japanese flowering quinces, lilacs, mock-oranges, and spireas. Pruning is needed to remove suckers from the base of several kinds of trees and shrubs—crab apples, lilacs, lindens, maples, and grafted plants, as fruit trees and roses.

In the case of girdling tree roots—those which grow over the main root system at the base of the trunk (generally visible)—pruning is needed to cut them where they are causing damage, and for this an ax may be needed. Don't overlook tree branches that block views or interfere with pedestrian or vehicular traffic around the house and garden. Sometimes branches get in the way of wires, or there is danger that big branches may break and fall on the roof. If so, get rid of them.

The correct time to prune spring-flowering shrubs, as forsythias, Japanese flowering quinces, Korean azaleas, deutzias, and lilacs, is after flowering is past. If too much is done early, much bloom will be lost. Yet some pruning is needed in the early spring to shape and eliminate unwanted wood. Wait for buds to break on those that start growth late, as black locust, catalpa, fringe tree, mulberry, and rose of sharon. Also wait for those that are apt to die practically to the ground, as blue hydrangea, butterfly bush, or vitex. Don't worry about cutting off blooms as they appear on the current season's growth.

*Closeup of yew branch pruned drastically in early spring,
showing new shoots on July 10. Yews can take hard pruning.*

Get to know if your clematis flowers on the old or current growth, as
there are two classifications. The common species anemone clematis
(*Clematis montana*) and its form pink anemone clematis (*C. m. rubra*)
bloom on old wood, as do varieties Belle of Woking, Duchess of Edin-
burgh, La Lorraine, and Miss Bateman. Most hybrids, however, flower
on the new season's growth, among them Comtesse de Bouchard, Duchess of Albany, Mrs. Cholmondeley, Nelly Moser, and Ramona. Growth
starts early, and with kinds that flower on the new growth pruning can
be more drastic. With others, prune mostly dead and weak branches.
Usually there is plenty of both—characteristic of clematis.

With evergreens be less severe, doing a little early each spring, as already advised. This way size can be controlled, and you'll hardly notice
that pruning has been done after the new growth develops to fill in. With
broad-leaved kinds, as camellias, cherry laurels, hollies, mahonias, mountain laurels, and rhododendrons, more thought and skill are required.
Again the same rule applies: do a little each spring and again after
flowering is past. If straggly shoots are present on formal evergreen
hedges—as boxwoods, hollies, or yews—clip to give a neat appearance
but do the major pruning in midsummer after the new growth has hardened. As a rule, formal evergreen hedges need one main shearing a year
except for straggly shoots that appear here and there.

# 9

## Important Lawn Care

OF ALL ASPECTS of gardening the lawn requires the most care to be healthy, without weeds, free of pests and diseases, and green even in time of droughts. A good lawn is the result only of one thing: tender, loving care. An established lawn, no matter how well cared for, very rarely comes through a northern winter without needing some early spring repair. Seeding, feeding, rolling, weed and pest control, and sodding are some of these, not to mention that early spring is a good time to start a new lawn.

Droughts and snow mold weaken lawns, making it virtually impossible for the healthiest turf to reach spring unscathed. There are some areas that always seem to die, mostly where shade is dense as grass tends to be weakest there. Poor drainage makes grass infirm, so winterkilling follows.

Snow mold is a turf disease—*Typhula itona*—sometimes called typhula blight. A common fungus, it thrives at low temperatures and spreads quickly when humidity is high and the thermometer hovers around forty degrees. The disease is fostered by a heavy blanket of snow that stays on the ground several weeks, but the results are not noticeable until the snow recedes and winter is over. Snow mold appears in patches, thick and cottony, and if not badly affected, grass may recover. Otherwise, it turns light brown or tan in color, contrasting with the green grass around it. Snow mold may also appear with snow, nurtured by humid weather and a high moisture content in the ground. The fungus is also more prevalent on bent grasses.

Snow itself followed by ice and rain can form a thick layer that lasts for weeks, smothering the grass beneath. Low areas are particularly susceptible to attack because water congregates and freezes causing the grass to mat. Slopes, where water rolls away and sun and air act as drying agents, are hardly touched.

Brown patch is a disease that attacks lawns in hot, humid summer weather, more common on thick, healthy, well-fed and watered turf in the heat of August. Enclosed gardens with poor drainage and circulation are

Dandelions can be dug from lawns with a manual weeder, but be careful to get out all the roots.

Where dandelions are abundant, particularly on large lawns, use a weed killer, as effective Weed-B-Gon.

more afflicted. Be sure not to overfeed, to avoid soft, succulent growth. Another preventive measure is to keep cutting grass into October and November, as long as it continues to grow. A chemical aid, Thiram, can be applied in late fall before snow appears. The systemic fungicide Benlate can be put down in the early spring to help counteract brown patch.

You may have no choice but to clean up the infested areas and reseed or plant sod. If there are bare spots in your lawn, replace them as early in spring as you can. Remember that grass seed can be sown any month of the year, even over snow since it can work its way down to the soil when the snow recedes.

If the damage is bad, you may need a shovel, spading fork, or power equipment, which can be rented. Shallow areas can be loosened with a metal rake. If grass has grown poorly in past years, it is advisable to remove old soil and bring in new. Then determine how much seed, fertilizer, and lime you will need. Weed killers can also be applied. Various kinds are available, some needing to be spread as much as two or more weeks before the seed can be sown. Follow directions for the kind you decide to buy. There are effective pre-emergent and postemergent killers for crab grass. Pre-emergents are spread in spring before lilacs come into

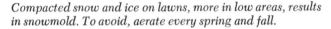

*Compacted snow and ice on lawns, more in low areas, results in snowmold. To avoid, aerate every spring and fall.*

bloom. Postemergents after the weed has made its appearance. No matter what chemical you use—and this pertains to spraying—always read directions carefully. It can make the difference between curing plants and killing them.

When removing soil, either because of snow mold, brown patch, or simply dead grass from ice compaction, never use peat moss, wood chips, or sand alone to fill the gaps, though these can be mixed with the soil to improve its texture. Work fertilizer and agricultural limestone to a depth of three to four inches before scattering seed—which should be of high quality, the kind best suited to your area. After seeding, roll and cover with a light mulch if you choose. Mulching is not necessary to growth, as the packing with the roller will bring the seed in contact with the soil. On slopes, where there is the problem of erosion, use hay mulch to hold the soil down and prevent the seed from washing away.

After seeding, spray with a mist of the nozzle or a light sprinkler three to four times a day. Merely spraying the surface suffices until germination. The idea is not to allow the surface to dry out, but after that, water more deeply. When growth is about two inches high, mow, setting the blades at one and a half inches, but do not allow grass to grow taller, as the mower will pull it when you cut it for the first time.

*Bare areas in lawns, killed by brown patch or snowmold,*
*can be filled with sod, a quick, easy way to have new grass.*

*Before laying sod, which comes rolled, dig dead grass and soil so sod will be level with the soil surrounding it.*

Another method for repairing bare areas is to sod. This is becoming more and more popular, even to the extent of making entire new lawns with sod, expensive at the start but less costly at the end. Sodding gives quick, overnight results. With it there is no digging of the soil to a great depth, except to remove some to accommodate the strips of sod; no seeding or watering; no waiting. Besides, weeds hardly present a problem at all, as good sod is already weed-free. Sod is also especially recommended for difficult areas, as the shade of trees, slopes, and areas that receive a lot of tramping from children and other members of the family.

As a rule, strips of sod are one or two feet wide and one to two inches thick. Sod need not be thick, but uniformity is important. Sod comes rolled for easy handling. Check strips you buy by unrolling them to be certain grass is not yellow inside, an occurrence when sod is kept rolled too long on the nursery grounds. To lay, dig the soil to the desired depth, tilling or cultivating the upper four to six inches. Scatter a high-nitrogen fertilizer, as 10-6-4, or fifteen to twenty pounds per one thousand square feet. Rake fertilizer into the soil and then roll.

Before laying sod, moisten soil but avoid making it wet or muddy. Fill in the cracks or openings with light soil or a mixture of soil and peat moss. To make certain each piece is firm and level, press with the hands or feet. If uneven, lift and place soil underneath. When sodding is finally completed, firm with a lightweight roller or the feet and sweep the sur-

Small lawn areas, as in city gardens, can be fertilized by hand. Scatter high nitrogen food evenly, then water in well.

Small bare patches in lawns can be seeded in early spring after removing old soil and replacing with new mixture.

*Do not try growing sun-loving grass in shade of large trees, such as this low branching beech, where pachysandra succeeds. Ground covers need feeding and watering because of tree roots.*

face with an old broom so soil will settle between cracks. If necessary, add more soil in openings among cracks. Water well with a sprinkler. If weather is dry keep soil moist, as grass will require a few weeks for roots to penetrate and become established.

On slopes, after preparing the soil, lay strips starting at the base and working up. As each piece is positioned, press firmly. A heavy board or the back end of a large shovel can be used. Until rooted, pieces of sod may slide down the slope during heavy rains. To avoid, insert pieces of low wire fencing into the soil about six inches at the base of each piece of sod, leaving the upper half sticking out. Remove when sod is well established.

Other pointers on lawns to keep in mind: apply the weed killer 2,4-D to destroy dandelions, plantain, chickory, and other broad-leaved weeds, following directions for use. Weeds are easily removed with hand weeders on small lawns, and if practiced throughout the summer and fall, the turf will be free of weeds.

To feed an established lawn use a high-nitrogen combination, usually applied at the rate of ten to twenty pounds per one thousand square feet. Small lawns can be fed by hand; large will need a spreader. If using an inorganic fertilizer, do not apply when grass is wet as it will burn. After scattering to dry turf, water thoroughly.

As warm weather approaches, adjust mowers to cut grass higher, one and one-half to two inches high, as this will shade roots and help retain moisture. If the lawn is mowed on the average of once a week, except in a wet spring, clippings can be left on the ground to become humus and provide some nitrogen.

Rolling is not necessary every year. A lawn rolled too often becomes compacted, cutting out air from the roots. If you feel your lawn needs to be rolled, do so in early spring when soil is moist, but not wet. Best rollers are those that are not too heavy, enough to press grass, pushed out of the soil by the alternating freezing and thawing of the soil in winter, into place.

If using a urea-type fertilizer, highly recommended for lawns, cut the number of applications in half, since the nitrogen is released slowly and evenly. Finally, where grass is next to impossible to grow in the thick shade of large maples, oaks, beeches, and other trees, plant ground covers—ajuga, English ivy, myrtle, pachysandra, or variegated goutweed. Or try taller-growing baneberries, ferns, Solomon's seal, or summer bleeding hearts if you want height.

# 10

## Planting Time for Trees and Shrubs

LIKE FALL, spring is planting time for woody plants—trees, shrubs, and vines. Tender kinds, as blue hydrangea and vitex in the North, and others doubtfully hardy, can be set out without fear of winterkilling. Where temperatures go well below freezing these plants are treated as perennials, in that new growth comes up from the roots each spring.

In spring you can put in bare-rooted plants, less expensive when sold this way. If you purchase plants through mail order houses, this is the way they come—leafless and without soil—as they are lighter and less costly to handle. Roots, of course, are wrapped in sphagnum moss or another medium to keep them moist. Evergreens, both needle and broadleaved, are sold in every season with a ball of earth because they are in leaf. If the ball of soil is not wrapped with burlap or plastic, plants are sold in tin, plastic, or other containers, so it is a simple matter to shift them to the garden without disturbing the root system.

The techniques of planting trees and shrubs, along with vines, do not differ widely from those recommended for the fall. Yet there is one major difference, namely, that with warm weather following you do not have to be concerned with dying. And you can plant anything, the very hardy, the partially so, the tender, the questionable.

Planting a tree, shrub, or vine must be done with care. Taking the extra effort will pay off, and it's all a matter of knowing—and applying—the basic principles. Read Chapter 7 in Part 1 for the techniques of soil preparation, planting, and early care.

Early spring is the time to give serious thought to foundation plantings, those next to and around the house. For the most part they are unattractive eyesores, clipped and sheared into spheres and squares, and yet they are the most important part of the garden design. No matter how much instruction and guidance garden writers and landscape architects offer in print, it seems to go unheeded. No matter where you go, it is difficult, if not impossible, to find a good foundation planting. A good garden, yes. Attractive plantings around the house, no. Early spring is a

*Eighteen-year-old rhododendron Boule de Neige after pruned on April 7, with cuttings—without flower buds—on the ground.*

*Rhododendron Boule de Neige after pruned a second time on May 23 when in bloom. Pruning can be done after blooming.*

*Closeup of cut branch of rhododendron Boule de Neige with new sprouts from latent buds stimulated by heavy pruning.*

*Same rhododendron as it appeared with new, lush growth on November 23 of the same year. Pruning is needed annually.*

time to re-evaluate these plantings, to do them right, to replace specimens that are too large to prune and bring back to proper proportion
and size.

Perhaps you have moved into a new house or your plantings are in
need of a face-lift. For best results, engage a landscape architect to draw
up a suitable plan that you can achieve yourself. If you cannot hire an
architect, take the time to really study the design of your plantings and
decide what you can afford to replace, perhaps over a period of a few
years. The biggest flaw is usually in overgrown front yards that need re-
modeling. Though some plants can be pruned and revived—deciduous
kinds are easier than evergreen—the best solution is to pull out old plants
and put in new ones. To keep foundation plants in good shape and proper

*Newly built house as it appeared in spring before planting
was started. All the work was performed by high school boys.*

*Preparing the soil along the foundation comprised deep digging with spading fork, then adding food and peat moss.*

*Same house as it appeared on August 25 of the same season, with a border of celosias and other annuals along the wall.*

*Balled and burlapped Japanese pieris ready for planting in eary spring. Plants are offered this way all season long.*

*Pebbles and large stones around a lamppost add interest and reduce upkeep, though leaves must be gathered in the fall.*

scale, they need annual pruning, sometimes twice as with rhododendrons, among the most difficult to keep small and graceful. Usually it takes a new foundation planting two or three years to fill out and become attractive. Neglected longer than this, corrective pruning becomes difficult, often impossible with some evergreens, as large spruces and hemlocks.

The front of the house needs some evergreens for year-round effect. They are especially needed at doorways and to soften the harsh corners of the house. The entranceway, traditional or contemporary, can be framed by a pair of choice evergreens. If the doorway is not centered but to one side, a single well-grown specimen will call attention to it without overdramatizing. At corners taller shrubs are needed to break the severe lines of the house. With tall houses, small flowering trees, as crab apples, dogwoods, fringe trees, or laburnums, will fill the need. Around the trunk, group low evergreens or deciduous shrubs—convex-leaved Japanese holly, dwarf azaleas, dwarf junipers and yews, Japanese flowering quinces, mountain pieris, mugo pine, and slender deutzia.

On a bank along the sidewalk or the driveway rely on ground covers to hold back the soil—English ivy, large-leaved vinca where hardy, myrtle, pachysandra, and variegated goutweed excellent in deep shade. The taller yellowroot is another excellent candidate. Then use ground covers in the shade of large trees in front of the house where grass is difficult to grow. They require some amount of care as weeds creep in, mostly just after planting, and plants need trimming, feeding, watering, and sometimes spraying. Nowadays, crushed stones or pebbles are taking their place, requiring less care, but be on the lookout for weeds and pull as soon as they appear. Or you might prefer an organic mulch—wood chips, shredded bark, or other material—with a shade-loving fern or hosta to break the monotony. Here again, weeds will invade, but care compared to grass or ground covers is next to nothing.

# 11

## Spring Care of Roses

WHEN IT COMES TO ROSES, there are two important spring needs. One is uncovering, pruning, and feeding plants protected for the winter; the other is planting, pruning, and feeding newly set plants. Both must be done early, when the weather moderates and after snow has disappeared. Early planting refers only to bare-rooted plants, as those in containers can be set out later when in leaf or in flower.

First, of course, comes uncovering. As with mulches, watch the weather carefully and look for bud swelling. When this starts you must get to work. Another indication that you can uncover roses is that the soil around them is soft and workable, and this applies to hybrid tea and other roses that have been hilled for the winter. Frozen soil cannot be taken away. If a crust is present, it is best to leave plants alone.

With hilled roses or those with plastic collars or Fiberglas Rose-bush Winterizers, first remove the mulch, if any. Then take away the extra soil with a shovel and a trowel. Both collars and winterizers can be washed with the hose, allowed to dry, then rolled neatly to be stored for reuse again in the late fall. Spraying canes (also wash them with the hose to remove mold) with a fungicide and insecticide is recommended as it helps prevent the recurrence of black spot, mildew, and other diseases, as well as insect eggs that may have overwintered in the soil or on the canes.

Then prune, first eliminating damaged, diseased, and dead wood. What is dead is brown in color, and if in doubt, leave until vigorous growth starts and you will know if certain canes or twigs should be cut. Remove suckers, growth from below the graft, branches that cross or are overcrowded, along with a few in the centers to let in more air and sun. Use sharp pruning shears or other tools, and make diagonal cuts, with the high side on the bud facade. Pruning height is a matter of taste when it comes to hybrid teas, floribundas, and grandifloras, as well as miniatures. High pruning—two feet or more—means taller plants with more but smaller blooms, and that seems to be the current trend. Years ago the

Planting a packaged bare-rooted hybrid tea rose in early spring. Plants are offered this way only when not in leaf.

Hybrid tea rose, variety Mirandy, with root system shown against shovel. Proper soil preparation precludes success.

*After planting, tamp to eliminate air, water, then mulch with organic matter. Prune to cut dead and excessive wood.*

*Climbing roses require much care in the spring. Prune early before buds swell and fasten to their supports as necessary.*

*Remove rose-bush winterizers, as shown in Part I, Chapter 6,*
*in early spring, being careful not to snap any of the branches.*

practice was to prune hard and severely, under a foot. This resulted in fewer but larger blooms.

As a rule, climbers are not covered except in severest climates, where canes are bent over and covered with an airy mulch or litter. To prune them, cut weak and diseased wood first. If large old canes have been killed to the ground, as they often are, seal the cuts with tree-wound paint. Equally important is securing canes to their supports as invariably some get disengaged with winter snow. So tie them with soft string, Twist-ems, or whatever else you are in the habit of using, provided it does not cut or bruise the stems. If growth is too dense, remove some live canes to open up, recommended if the background—a wall, fence, or trellis—is an attractive one.

Once roses have been uncovered, pruned, and tied back, they should be fed, using a complete fertilizer according to directions. Add some organic matter (such as peat moss, compost, dehydrated manure, wood chips, or shredded bark) which will act as a summer mulch, keeping the soil cool and helping prevent excessive growth of weeds. Feeding can be done with a crowbar, a root feeder, or hand trowel in the case of bush roses. Usually a shrub type needs one-half to one cup of mixed fertilizer, worked lightly into the soil with a trowel or cultivated. Water if the weather is dry, as moisture is needed to activate fertilizer.

You may be planting some roses in the early spring. No matter how many bushes you have, roses have a way of dying under the best of winter protection conditions, and hybrid teas are most known for this tendency. Even if none have died, you may want to try some of the new varieties or some that are new to you. Plants ordered through catalogues will arrive bare-rooted, wrapped in plastic or coarse paper, with moist sphagnum moss. Keep them in a cool place, as the garage, until ready to plant. No matter what kind you select, remember roses need sun for at least half a day.

*After rose-bush winterizers are taken off, remove the soil carefully with a hand trowel, then cut string and prune.*

*The last step is to feed the roses. Scatter a mixed food around crowns, dig in with trowel, and water if it is dry.*

To plant roses, dig the soil deeply, turning it over thoroughly, and keep the good topsoil in a pile at one side. For bare-rooted plants, the hole should be eighteen inches across and at least a foot deep, better a foot and a half. Mix peat moss, leafmold, compost, dry manure, or other organic matter at the bottom of the hole. Make a mound of soil in the center, resting the plant on it, with the graft an inch or two below the level of the ground, spreading the roots out in all directions. Add some topsoil, tamp with the hands or feet, and scatter a handful or two of mixed fertilizer, like 5-10-5, or a rose food at the outer edges of the hole, not in the center.

Water well, and after it seeps in add more soil, pressing to firm and eliminate air. Use the rest of the soil, mounding some to a height of six or eight inches to protect plants from the drying effects of sun and wind. Remove and level off the soil when leaves appear and then leave a slight depression to hold water. Lastly, do not forget to mulch. When plants leaf out fully scatter another handful or two of fertilizer at the perimeter.

*If plastic rose collars are used, remove and take the soil away with a trowel. Then follow with feeding and pruning.*

If bare-rooted plants arrive before you are ready to set them out or weather does not permit, remove the heavy paper, plastic, or foil. Dig in the ground, preferably a shady spot, or insert in buckets of water for three or four days. The water will make stems plump again if they have shriveled somewhat in shipping.

Although container roses come in well-prepared soil, your soil preparation in the garden is the same as for bare-rooted plants. A hole about a foot across generally suffices, but the mound of earth in the center is not needed. When ready to plant, turn over the tin, rip the papier-mâché container or slip the rose out of the plastic container, keeping soil and roots intact. With tin cans, you may have to cut them along two sides with strong, metal-cutting shears. Heavy shears will slit plastic easily, but with papier-mâché make a tear at the top edge, pull down, and it will rip open.

In order not to disrupt the root ball, hold the base of the plant firmly with one hand and place the other under the ball of soil. Place carefully in position, adding soil, water, fertilizer as instructed for bare-rooted specimens. If in leaf, these roses will not need mounding, but spread out coiled roots around the edges of the root ball. Be gentle with tamping so the root ball will stay intact. Prune to remove unwanted wood, but if in doubt, wait until buds break and new strong growth appears.

# 12

## How to Handle Perennials

EARLY BLOOMING PERENNIALS are best lifted and separated in the fall when they are in a dormant state. Late bloomers, on the other hand, are so treated in the early spring just as growth starts. Because they flower in summer and fall they have ample time to become well-established. Late bloomers divided in the spring include chrysanthemums, fall asters, Japanese anemones, heleniums, helianthus, monkshoods, phlox, and rose-mallow. Early bloomers, for fall lifting and dividing, include bearded iris, bleeding hearts, blue phlox, columbines, doronicums, gold-dust, lupines, primroses, and Virginia bluebells.

The lifting, separating, and planting procedure is roughly the same as that outlined in the perennial chapter in Part 1. The spring offers one advantage: More fertilizer and organic matter can be applied because of the warm weather and vigorous growth that follows. In the fall you do not want to stimulate late growth, unable to harden properly before cold weather.

Perennials that are not to be lifted will need minimum care. Shallow-rooted kinds, as bearded iris and chrysanthemums, often heaved out of the ground as a result of frost action, should be pressed in with the feet. Then scatter a mixed fertilizer according to directions, scratching soil lightly with a cultivator or spade. Water if the soil is dry. Apply a mulch —your favorite material, preferably organic, as peat moss, leafmold, shredded bark, or wood chips. Needless to say, clean all remaining foliage that was not taken away in the fall. Also cut to the ground stems that were allowed to remain during winter.

Perennials are classified in yet two other groups: those that spread and need frequent dividing and those that do not like to be disturbed and can remain in the same spot for several years, peonies being the most notable example. To maintain vigor and profuse bloom, spreaders need separating every two or three years—four at the most. Kinds in this category include anthemis, arabis, astilbes, bearded iris, bee-balms, blue, ground, and perennial phlox, boltonias, campanulas, cerastiums, chrysanthemums,

*Early spring is the time to lift and divide early flowering perennials, as phlox, into sections with three to four shoots.*

coral-bells, dianthus, doronicums, fall asters, gaillardias, gold-dust, heleniums, helianthus, lamb's ears, primroses, shasta daisies, stokesias, veronicas, and yarrows. With most of these spreaders the outer shoots are the youngest, the most vigorous, the ones to retain for replanting, discarding the outworn inner, often dead centers.

Those that do not require disturbance include aconitums, amsonias, armerias, asclepias, baby's-breath, balloonflowers, baptisias, bleeding hearts, Christmas roses, cimicifugas, daylilies, echinops, gasplants, hostas, liatris, lupines, Oriental poppies, peonies, scabiosas, sedums, thalictrums, and thermopsis.

Several other pointers ought to be kept in mind regarding perennials in early spring. If any are covered with a mulch or winter blanket, watch the weather carefully. If it warms quickly, premature soft growth may be stimulated. The best method is to loosen the mulch and keep it to one side so it can be replaced in the event of sudden cold weather.

If plants are to be lifted and divided or new ones set out, be certain the ground is dry enough. Take a handful of soil, squeeze it lightly, and if it stays in a lump without falling or breaking apart, it is not dry enough to handle. If planting or replanting large areas or complete borders, scatter agricultural lime just before the ground is spaded as this will sweeten sour soil and increase bacterial action. It is advisable to spread lime among perennials where annuals are grown as well every three to four years. Lime also makes heavy soils lighter and sandy and porous soils compact.

If you are doing little or no dividing, cultivate the soil after spreading the fertilizer so it can get into the soil and begin to work. Be careful not to break any tips as new growth is soft, tender, and succulent. In the fall label those that sprout late in the spring—balloonflowers, Japanese anemones, plumbagos, and rosemallows—so you will not think they are dead and pull them up. After cleaning, feeding, and watering, insert twiggy branches—as those of birch—around plants to support stems, a

*When setting out divisions of phlox or other perennials, first prepare soil with organic matter and fertilizer.*

*After placing phlox divisions in position, firm with hands and water thoroughly. Keep moist when weather is very dry.*

method widely practiced in the British Isles. It will save much effort later when staking. Growth that develops is natural and graceful, lacking the stiff appearance of plants that are rigidly staked.

It is important that dead leaves be removed from around hollyhocks to check rust, a common disease that turns leaves orange-brown in summer. Spray them with ferbam or dust with sulphur. Peonies suffer botrytis blight, and so it is imperative that old leaves be removed and new red shoots be sprayed with Bordeaux or zineb every ten days, three times, starting when shoots are just a few inches high.

If you have a cold-frame, you can start seeds of perennials as well as annuals four weeks ahead of planting time outdoors, even sooner in warm parts of the country where early spring frosts are not apt to occur. Seedlings of all kinds, including tomatoes and other vegetables, can be transferred to cold-frames or hotbeds, thinning and separating them to allow enough space for each to develop properly. On warm days open cold-frames so plants, whatever kinds, will harden properly.

You'll have to give bearded iris special attention if you suspect they have borers, a difficult pest to control. Once imbedded inside rhizomes they cannot be reached with chemical sprays. First get rid of all old leaves, which should be done both in late fall and early spring. Here eggs of the moths are present, and larvae eat their way into rhizomes, staying there all season.

After cleaning, spray to control the iris borer. Use a two per cent lindane dust or a lindane spray once a week, starting when leaves are a few inches high until June 1. Do not apply to foliage but use only around plants. Lindane, legal for all kinds of borers, will check this pest on dogwoods, lilacs, and other woody plants. Apply to barks only.

You may have difficult areas in your garden where you wonder what kinds of perennials will do best. Sunny with light, dry, sandy soil? Then consider arabis, artemisias, balloonflowers, baptisias, bearded iris, blue flax, coreopsis, daylilies, dianthus, echinops, evening primroses, gaillardias, gloriosa daisies, gold-dust, lavender, lupines, pyrethrums, rudbeckias, sedums, thermopsis, thymes, verbascums, yarrows, and yuccas.

A wet, moist spot? Then grow astilbes, bee-balms, cardinal flowers, chelones, cimicifugas, doronicums, filipendulas, heleniums, Japanese iris, loosestrifes (*Lythrum*), primroses, meadow-rues, rosemallows, and Virginia bluebells.

In shade you have a wide choice—aconites, ajugas, astilbes, bleeding hearts, blue phlox, Christmas roses, cimicifugas, columbines, daylilies, epimediums, eupatoriums, foxgloves (biennial), hostas, iberis, primroses, pulmonarias, saxifragas, thalictrums, trollius, violas, and Virginia bluebells.

# 13

## Preparing the Vegetable Garden
## for Early Spring

TODAY GROWING VEGETABLES is an important aspect of home gardening. Millions of Americans are growing their own not only to beat inflation but to enjoy vegetables of better quality. To get the most from your time and effort, always start with a plan, one that can be worked out in the winter or in the very early spring before actual planting starts. Then you will know what you are doing and not waste time and effort.

If you prepared the soil of your vegetable garden in the fall—the ideal time—in spring you only need to cultivate it a little, making it easier to sow seed or set out young plants. Then scatter and scratch in some mixed fertilizer, as well as any organic matter, like dry manure or compost.

If you did not till your soil and add lime in the fall, do it in the early spring. In fact, with light, very sandy soils, digging is best postponed to early spring, while heavy or clayey soils are better plowed in the fall. If you sowed a green manure crop of annual rye, buckwheat, or alfalfa, it will need to be turned under with a tiller or spading fork as soon as the ground is workable. Do this as soon as possible, at least a month in advance of planting in order to give the organic matter a chance to partially decompose.

Make sure the soil, whether using a rototiller (a mechanical tiller that does a better job, so it is worth renting for a day) or a spading fork, is loosened to a depth of at least six inches. Eight or ten inches are better, especially for root crops, as beets, carrots, and turnips. Since vegetables like a friable soil that crumbles easily, loosen it by adding organic matter —peat moss, wood chips, compost, or whatever—to the depth at which it is dug. The organic matter improves the texture of the soil, helps retain moisture, and adds a degree of nutrients. After working in the organic matter, wait about a week before raking and smoothing so it will have a chance to settle and start to decay. Then spread the balanced fertilizer before raking. As a group, vegetables are tolerant of a wide range of soils —just about all kinds, except soil that tends to stay soggy or wet much of

*First step in growing vegetables is turning over the soil
Easiest way is a rototiller, though a spading fork will do.*

*After soil has been plowed, scatter mixed fertilizer and
rake to even out before sowing seed or setting out plants.*

*Cold-frame with several kinds of luttuce opened for plants to harden off. If spaced sufficiently apart, plants can be harvested in the cold-frame, thus producing an early crop.*

the time. Follow directions for portions of fertilizer, but an average amount consists of fifty pounds of a balanced fertilizer per one thousand square feet.

Examples of a balanced fertilizer are 5-10-5, 4-12-4, 10-10-10, and 20-20-20. The first number represents nitrogen, the second phosphoric acid, and the third potash. Avoid only lawn fertilizers that are not balanced but have a high percentage of nitrogen. The nitrogen promotes leaf growth, indicated by the first of the three numbers. Work the fertilizer into the upper inch or so of soil with the tiller, spading fork, or plow. The first feeding is applied when the soil is tilled. The second and last should be given as plants start to grow—when they are about four inches high. Scatter and scratch in the food two to three inches away from the stems, a form of feeding known as side dressing.

Usually the first feeding—at tilling time—is applied in dry form. The second can be given in dry or liquid form, making the latter more quickly available to the roots. As with all plants, feed only soil that is moist, otherwise burning might result. No other food is necessary, particularly for vegetables such as eggplants, peppers, and tomatoes, which are grown for their fruits. Too much feeding—particularly too much nitrogen —induces lush leaf growth with few and small fruits.

After soil has been prepared you may be bothered by animal pests— cats, dogs, skunks, and woodchucks—which try to dig it up. If possible, fence in the entire area. Where there are no small children, scatter moth- balls to discourage these pests. Where children play, substitute moth flakes as they are lest apt to be picked up. They need replacing periodi- cally.

Remember that watering is an important part of gardening success. Seed sown close to the surface will need daily sprinkling, even twice a day if the weather is hot. As vegetables grow, water to a depth of several inches, at least six. It is better to give one weekly deep soaking than sev- eral surface sprinklings during the course of the week, as this merely draws roots upward in search of moisture. Needless to say, apply a

*When first vegetables appear or are planted, the vegetable garden can be mulched, as with shredded bark or compost. This will keep moisture in soil and help to check weeds.*

*Tray with Large White Globe Onion started indoors March 19 by watering through punctured holes. Picture taken April 17. Below, same onion plants on April 19 after some of the seedlings had been transplanted to another tray.*

mulch after young plants are a few inches high to conserve moisture and help control weeds. Straw, marsh hay, shredded bark, leaves, grass clippings, layers of newspapers, or sheets of plastics are some of the best choices.

The question of soil acidity often comes up. Most vegetables prefer a slightly acid soil, one ranging from a pH of 6 or 6.5 to 7. Those more tol-

*One tray of Large White Globe Onion, showing how much the transplanted seedlings had developed by May 17, when they were photographed. After, all were set out in the garden.*

erant of a slightly acid soil include eggplants, peppers, potatoes, sweet potatoes, tomatoes, and watermelons. Less tolerant are asparagus, cauliflower, celery, leeks, lettuce, onions, and spinach. Soil can be tested for acidity by sending samples to your agricultural experiment station. Soil-testing kits with detailed instructions may be purchased at garden centers so you can test your own regularly. Agricultural lime applied in correct amounts makes acid soil more alkaline.

For the most part, seed should not be sown outdoors until soil has warmed up, though some vegetables can take cold and can be planted earlier. Beets, for example, can be planted as soon as the ground is *workable* though not entirely warm. Others to sow early include quick-maturing radishes, which do not like hot weather; peas, known for their preference for coolness; lettuce, likewise a cool-weather crop; onions, spinach, turnips, early carrots, Swiss chard, and parsnips to mention a few others.

Hot-weather vegetables, which must be sown or set out as young

*Tomato Early Girl, started in Jiffy-7 Miracle Pots indoors in a sunny south window April 25, were photographed May 18.*

*Young seedlings of tomato Early Girl were transferred to separate pots in light soil on May 19, still kept indoors.*

*Early Girl tomatoes, still in their individual pots inside, had grown this much and were staked. Photo taken June 6.*

*Pots were placed in ground outdoors for them to harden off in an eastern exposure before setting in open soil.*

*Four plants of tomato Early Girl, planted in same spot after soil was properly prepared, developed this much by July 2.*

*Plants, grown this height by July 21, mingled with Blaze climbing rose, blue hydrangea, and Carolina rhododendron.*

*The first tomato ripened on August 25. When photographed
on September 6 there were many fruits. By frost 86 in all.*

plants when the ground is thoroughly warm and all danger of frost has passed, include cucumbers, lima beans, New Zealand spinach, okra, peppers, pumpkins, squashes, and tomatoes.

After seedlings appear comes the necessary task of thinning. Directions for each type of vegetable are given on the seed packet, so save it after planting. For example, carrots require a spacing of about two inches; beets, two to three inches; and beans, four to five inches.

For earlier crops some seeds can be sown indoors in sunny windows, in the cold-frame or hotbed, or in the greenhouse. These include beets, broccoli, cabbage, celery, early lettuce, eggplants, peppers, sweet potatoes, and tomatoes. Most vegetables fortunately do not mind transplanting, among them beets, broccoli, cauliflower, eggplants, kale, lettuce, onions, and peppers. Celery, Brussels sprouts, Swiss chard, and tomatoes are others. A few suffer if transplanted, including corn, cucumbers, lima beans, melons, and watermelons, but they can be raised in pots. Many people who raise vegetables buy young plants, either in flats —the most popular method—or in individual small pots from nurseries or garden centers in the spring. This is handy, time saving, and easier if facilities—and time—are lacking. It is also advisable for those who have small vegetable garden plots or grow plants in containers on rooftops.

A few pointers to keep in mind: (1) As with flower gardening, it is not size that counts, but quality. Determine how much area you can handle efficiently, remembering it is better to have a good, small vegetable garden than one that is too large and ill kept. (2) As much as possible, practice rotation. Many vegetables do not do well if grown in the same spot year after year, even if fed. In planting, keep tall kinds—as pole beans and tomatoes—at the back with medium and small kinds in front. If the vegetable plot is in the middle of the lawn, then place taller vegetables in rows in the center, with smaller ones at sides. (3) Do not underestimate the value of organic matter. Balanced fertilizers cannot take its place, so add some each spring—or fall—and mulch with organic material at least once. Two or three times is even better as organic material decomposes to go back into the soil, enrich it, and make it possible to grow better and tastier vegetables.

# 14

## Don't Neglect Herbs

THE FIRST STEP in growing herbs, either for flavoring foods, scent, or ornament, is to distinguish perennials from annuals and treat each according to its own needs. Hardy perennials—bergamot, mints, and tansy—die to the ground, so their tops should be cut to this point in the fall. If it was not done then, be sure to cut them early in spring. Many herbs are annuals—to be newly planted each year—and these include anise, borage, chervil, coriander, dill, sweet basil, sweet fennel—a perennial treated as an annual—sweet marjoram, and summer savory. Bee-balm, chives, horehound, horse-radish, lavender, lemon-balm, mints, rosemary, tarragon, and winter savory are perennials. Lemon verbena is a shrubby perennial, not hardy in colder regions, and the same applies to the rose and other kinds of scented geraniums. A few are biennial, among them caraway and parsley.

If you have mulched any of your herbs from last year, uncover and remove them when the ground becomes warm. In the cold North, sage and santolina often die without protection, unless they have been covered with a thick layer of snow. Next, check for dieback of uncovered herbs. Lavender, used as edging in rose gardens and in rockeries, may die back considerably. Clean it out with sharp pruning shears as soon as sprouts appear, so you know which portions are dead and which are not. In warmer parts of the country both lavender and sage are subshrubs. They spread widely, die back very little, but must be cleaned out when spring arrives.

Early spring is the best time to lift and separate perennial herbs, particularly those of questionable hardiness. It's the time to set out new plants you buy from nurserymen or garden centers. Later in the spring you can obtain flats of basil, parsley, and others to treat as annuals. You may want to start from seed, either directly in the open ground when it's warm enough, or in flats indoors in February, March, or April.

If you have stored herbs in a cold-frame, remember to open it on warm days to harden plants off and prevent soft growth. Cover again at

*Growing herbs is now very popular. What better way than a formal plot where you can grow the kinds you like most. Hardy perennials and annuals can be easily combined.*

night when the weather gets cold, and set out in their permanent positions after all danger of frost is past.

Culture is relatively simple. Most are easy to grow, if not winter hardy, requiring a light, well-drained not-too-rich soil and sun. Since they do not like an acid soil, add agricultural lime in the recommended amounts. Established plants can be given a light sprinkling with a mixed fertilizer, high in phosphorous, as 5-10-5 or 4-8-4. Better are bone meal and superphosphate, slow-acting phosphoric fertilizers that do not burn. Most herbs need sun at least half a day. Some herbs, particularly angelica, bee-balm, bergamot, costmary, mints, parsley, sweet ciceley, and sweet woodruff flourish in partial shade, even shade if cast by high-branching trees or buildings. A few will withstand deep shade—bloodroot, ginseng, foxglove (*Digitalis*), and snakeroot.

Lavender, lemon verbena, rosemary, and thymes prefer and tolerate

*A cherished herb is lavender grown for the aromatic scent of its spiked flowers and gray leaves. In cold regions it suffers from winterkilling. In spring prune dead portions.*

considerable dryness, while angelica, bergamot, lovage, mints, parsley, and sweet ciceley thrive in moist locations. However, be certain to water all kinds of herbs during periods of extended droughts.

Though herbs can be grown anywhere you like—in borders with shrubs, perennials, and annuals, in rock gardens, or in containers of many kinds—they look best in an herb garden where they are grown by themselves for use and beauty. Herb gardens are becoming more and more the vogue—that is, the formal, intricately designed herb garden, including the knot garden so much a part of Elizabethan England.

Traditional designs, including elaborate parterres, are often preferred by serious herb growers, though not practical for the typical homeowner. The more ambitious gardener can consult books on the subject, with their assortment of patterns. You can get ideas and inspiration by visiting herb gardens (many are open to the public) and botanical gardens, which invariably contain attractive formal herb gardens.

The herb garden, which can be started in the early spring, can be large or small. It need not be ornate—a tiny plot three or four feet square can contain several different kinds. The herb plot may be a narrow strip along the sunny side of the house or garage. It can be a simple geometric design somewhere in the garden—square, rectangular, triangular, circular, oval, or free-form. It can be a raised bed, with sides of brick, stone, concrete, or railroad ties.

*The usual place for the herb garden is by the kitchen door where snippets of parsley, mint, oregano, and others can be easily taken when preparing meals or refreshing beverages.*

The beginner will do better with a simple design, as intricate patterns require constant skilled care. If possible, locate near the kitchen door, where snippets can be gathered easily for cooking. Most of all, study up on herbs so you will get to know which are perennial, biennial, or annual. Learn their growth habits and ultimate heights. Include some for edging, as they lend neatness and frame the herb garden, whether simply or ornately designed. Study leaf textures and colors, remembering that most are gray or blue-green, though some are dark or light green. The large-leaved annual basil Dark Opal is red-purple in coloring and can be used for edging anywhere you like in the garden. Learn the various uses of herbs, how to flavor meats and fish, salads, soups, and drinks. Your gardening pleasure will be greater and your meals for the family and friends more interesting and pleasing.

# 15

## Early Outdoor Container Plants

YOU CAN GIVE your home and garden a heart-warming jump on spring with flowering plants already in bloom—pansies and Dutch bulbs—set out in window boxes, planters, tubs and pots, kettles, and even hanging containers. Many kinds of flowering plants are available from nurserymen and garden centers just as soon as the weather warms.

In the North, winter is the longest and dreariest of the seasons, stretching at least from November 1 to April 1. In some areas it's longer, with snow coming in October and lingering well into April. It does not matter whether you live in the suburbs, cities, or the open country. The lively splashes of color from early spring flowers are more welcome than the first crocus or robin, particularly in window boxes and other containers that soften and brighten the cold, hard surfaces of concrete and brick.

If you have window boxes, for your own pleasure remove the materials used to decorate them for the winter—the greens, red ruscus, strawflowers, bittersweet berries, silvered branches. If you did not paint them last fall, do it now when it is easier without plants in them. Change the soil if needed, or refurbish it with organic matter and fertilizer to be ready to plant, in the event the weather is still too chilly. Do the same with outside containers or others that you bring out of storage to plant for the season. Make certain all containers have drainage holes, and place crocks or stones at bottoms to allow water to run off.

The pansy is a beloved flower, with its delightful "faces," some that smile, others that frown, others shy or sad, some pert or saucy. What's more, it can withstand considerable cold, and overwinters as seedling plants in areas where temperatures go far below freezing. Florists and garden centers sell plants in full bloom so they will give pleasure immediately. They can be planted on their own and do not need companion plants. If you want another flower in the container, one of the best is forget-me-not, blue or lavender, cool loving and smaller so it will not de-

*Enjoy an advance on spring by planting Dutch bulbs, as tulips, along with English ivy as trailer in window boxes. Daffodils and hyacinths can be set out when heavy frost danger is past.*

tract from the pansies. The Swiss and other hybrid pansies are large flowering, but tend to bloom more sparsely than the smaller flowering varieties. The choice is up to you, also as to whether you prefer those with faces or solid hued kinds, like violas, in yellow, blue, and white.

Years ago hybrid English daisies in rose, deep and light pink, and white, were more popular than they are today, though they seem to be staging a comeback. Like pansies, they like cool weather and put on their best performance early in the season. With hot weather these two, along with forget-me-nots, languish and have to be removed and replaced with other flowers. Only in the coldest areas, where seasons are very short, do they last all summer, an envy of southern gardeners.

You can buy Dutch bulbs in bud form, just starting to break, in flats or pots for window boxes and other containers. Years ago this was unheard of. What, for example, can be more uplifting than window boxes filled with golden-yellow daffodils? Boxes can be planted a pale green, soft yel-

*An urn of tulips by a city doorway costs very little. When finished, other flowers, as geraniums, can be substituted.*

low, light blue, lavender, or white. Larger than pansies or English daisies, they are more dazzling. Blue forget-me-nots make ideal companion plants, not only for color but because they will carry on after the daffodils have faded and you are not yet ready to replace them. Daffodil foliage remains green a long time.

Hyacinths are probably the most fragrant early spring flower. Rose, pink, purple, blue, and white blend harmoniously, but others are available, as yellow and orange, to suit your taste. Bold flowers, they somehow seem best alone, except perhaps for a few forget-me-nots.

Tulips in all sizes and colors have become very popular as early spring container flowers. They can be mixed, tall, medium, and short, and both English daisies and forget-me-nots can be interspersed among them. In the cool weather of very early spring before tulips bloom in the open ground, these bulbs last a long time—as much as two weeks—as if kept in a florist's refrigerator. A day or two may be hot, but not evenings, which revive them and help continue their life span.

Another favorite, much grown as a bedding plant in Europe, is the sweetly fragrant wallflower. Wallflowers are often set out in the fall in the warmer parts of the country, where they are also planted in window boxes and other containers. Colors are many, chiefly yellow, orange, reddish brown, and mahogany.

The next group comprises plants that like cool weather, that become exhausted and give up with hot weather of June and July. Years ago these were not grown where summers are hot, but now they are forced, and so can be set out in early spring where they will flourish in cool weather. Included here are annual or drummond phlox; bachelor's-but-

*English daisies are delightful early spring flowers which thrive best in cool weather. Rose, pink, or white, hybrids are large flowering. Combine with blue forget-me-nots.*

tons, taller for the rear of window boxes; nasturtiums, including climbing types, often sold in pots attached to a tripod of bamboo stakes; primroses, which are perennials that can be transferred to the garden when faded; and violas in orange and blue.

Stock is still another cool-loving flower cherished for its delicate scent and now available in heat-resistant strains. Even so, it makes a good candidate for the early spring outdoor container. Two that are less known but worth a try are clarkia, which grows quickly from seed sown indoors, and the low, bushy nemesia—scarlet, rose, pink, blue, purple, yellow, orange, and white. It's a delightful annual, a charmer that never fails to attract attention because it is not very common.

*A ceramic strawberry jar is a choice garden novelty, not only for strawberries. Pansies can be planted for spring color, followed by sweet alyssum or a variety of fragrant herbs.*

*To prepare a window box properly for planting, first place crocks, stones, or other material over the drainage holes.*

*When placing soil in window boxes, use a mixture that is well supplied with humus, as peat moss, and a mixed food.*

*Climbing nasturtiums, which relish cool weather, and fragrant white carnations add a welcome note to a porch.*

For holidays, unless the weather is cold, blowy or snowy, make a grouping of container plants at your entranceway or doorway—a few stately Easter lilies, pink tulips, blue hyacinths and forget-me-nots, and, of course, the inevitable pansies. If frost threatens, they are easily lifted and taken indoors for the night. This applies to all containers that are not too heavy, even metal or plastic window boxes that are not secured, so they can be picked up from the outside if close to ground level or brought inside by opening the windows.

There are other annuals available early to set out in containers, but they are summer flowers that, to me, make no sense. These include plants of coleus, fuchsias, geraniums, lantanas, marigolds, patience plants, petunias, and snapdragons. Why plant them when you can have spring flowers instead? Besides, marigolds, petunias, and snapdragons become very tired looking by late August (you will become tired of them, too) if you set them out in April or early May, as some do. So begin with the others, true flowers of spring.

Available—all year around for that matter—are chrysanthemums, but I frown upon their use. Perhaps not to younger generations, but to the older they belong to autumn strictly, a flower that is associated with that season. Besides, after the chrysanthemums wither, what next? More chrysanthemums? If you do not start out with spring flowers, but plant geraniums, marigolds, and other summer flowers in May or June, you'll want to end up with chrysanthemums. Ideally, the procession should start with spring flowers as pansies and English daisies, then fuchsias and geraniums, ending finally with chrysanthemums, finishing the growing season with a bang.

If you do not want to bother with flowers, set out evergreens—small specimens in window boxes; larger, in tubs, urns, planters, or other appropriate containers. They are available as soon as they can be dug and can be planted immediately, cold weather or warm. Hardy, they are able to withstand whatever abnormal weather early spring might bring.

Large container plants—trees, shrubs, and evergreens—on terraces, rooftops, and decks, and at doorways can remain in the same container several years. In early spring they will need special care. One method is to remove with a trowel or small shovel several inches of old soil from the top and replace it with a fresh mixture, containing humus and fertilizer. In some cases, they can be merely fed, but all will need some pruning to control their size and to improve form and shape.

Containers with trees and shrubs that remain outdoors all winter—as wooden tubs and boxes, metal, and concrete—should be well-watered. Drying winds and sun take their toll, so water when the soil thaws in winter. Ample water is especially needed for plants close to the house, at both sides of the doorway, where little snow or rain is apt to reach them —winter or summer.

# Part Four

SCHEDULE FOR THE SOUTH

# 1

## Late Fall in the South

THE SOUTH, like the North, comprises a large part of the country. Separated by the Mason-Dixon line, it stretches from the Pacific Ocean to the Atlantic. Mexico is the only southern neighbor, and the Gulf Coast reaches from Texas to the Floridian Peninsula. The South possesses high elevations, as mountainous areas in Arizona and New Mexico and in Kentucky, Tennessee, and the Carolinas. France, the second largest country in Europe, is three-fourths the size of Texas. Only by consulting a zonal map (study the one in this book) can you know the high and low areas and the winter temperatures in each zonal area. Central sections are colder, and zonal areas in the interior dip southward as they do throughout the country. Only tiny sections in California and Texas and a larger area in southern Florida are generally free of frost, then not always. As a season, winter in the South is short, extending roughly from late November or early December to mid- or late March at the latest.

Actually no part of the United States is frost-free except the southern tip of Florida and Key West. Damage, often killing the citrus trees to the ground, is well known in California and Florida. Spring in the South comes slowly and less dramatically than in the North, though certain plants there flower all year.

In the South it's not so much a matter of "winterizing," though there are certain tasks which southern gardeners must perform in winter, some of them protection measures like lifting tender achimenes and caladium bulbs. Another is using heaters, indispensable for citrus fruit growers, and keeping hoses and sprinklers running all night when temperatures plummet below 32° F. The other alternative is to water palms and other tropical plants in the early morning to melt the ice and save them from excessive damage.

Winter starts when deciduous trees and shrubs start to shed their leaves. These are few, among them plane trees, dogwoods, mulberries, California pepper trees, and flowering almonds. Most are evergreen—

*In the warm South where leaves, as oleander, shed all year round, a cart like this will keep driveways and walks clean.*

camellias, citrus, eucalyptus, and oleanders—and they are constantly dropping leaves.

Rake, pick up, and dispose of excess leaves in one way or another, but do not destroy them. Since leaves are fewer, they are needed as mulch to place around trees, shrubs, and perennials or to relegate to the compost pile. With perennials, such as delphiniums and Oriental poppies and plants that retain green leaf rosettes all winter, avoid a too-thick cover as it can cause smothering. Leaves can also be used to protect tender plants from cold. In woodsy, naturalistic plantings, leaves may be allowed to stay where they fall. They will eventually decay and return to the soil, enriching it with humus and nutrients. Leaves of live oak are recommended because they are small and acid in content, excellent for azaleas, camellias, and other acid-loving plants. For small plants like perennials, pine needles are better, less apt to cause smothering as they permit air to reach crowns and roots.

Southern lawns require late-fall attention. Bermuda and cold climate grasses should be mowed as long as needed, often all winter long. Fall, when weeds die down, is a good time to feed lawns. When turf thickens and seed starts to germinate, weeds stand less chance of gaining foothold. Favorite grasses are Bermuda, St. Augustine, and zoysia.

If Bermuda grass starts to turn yellow, a lack of nitrogen is indicated. Apply a fertilizer combination with a high percentage of nitrogen. In winter, when weather is cooler, lawn mowers can be adjusted to increase the cutting height of the turf. Where warm enough (a common practice in warmer areas of Arizona) many gardeners sow annual rye seed over Bermuda grass in the late fall. It soon takes over, creating a lush, green carpet, then dies with the appearance of warm weather, when the Bermuda grass again becomes dominant. Since Bermuda grass often creeps over edges into shrub and flower borders, winter is a good time to cut it back or set out an edging of brick, stones, or other permanent material.

Trees and shrubs can be planted all winter in the Lower South. Kinds that can be set out include azaleas, camellias, Chinese hibiscus, citrus, crape-myrtles, eucalyptus, eugenias, gardenias, hollies, loquats, nandinas, oleanders, olives, and palms.

*Zoysia is a perennial creeping grass that is commonly used as a lawn substitute in the warmest parts of the country.*

*Crown-of-thorns in a Florida garden produces its gay, red "flowers" abundantly all year. White rounded stones show the plant off dramatically and help hold moisture in soil.*

Trees and shrubs need other care. One of these is spraying. One common pest—scale—found on camellias, citrus, gardenias, and oleanders, can be checked with malathion or emulsified oil, though the latter cannot be applied to evergreens where there is danger of freezing. Best leave oil spraying for the early spring and as always follow directions precisely. Dormant sprays, however, can be applied to dogwoods, flowering almonds, flowering peaches, lilacs, and other woody plants that are attacked by scale.

Watering is necessary particularly in the desert and near-desert areas. This is important in the Southwest if expected late fall rains do not appear. Mulching with gravel and stone chips, less apt to wash away in downpours, will help retain moisture. Through the winter watering may be needed. Rains in California come during the winter months and can cause rotting. For this reason good drainage is essential, so check it before winter sets in.

Fruits that are still making growth, such as apricots, cherries, nectarines, peaches, and bush fruits, may need extra water. It may also be required in California and other dry states where gardening—and farming—is largely dependent on irrigation. In winter, when it is cooler and there are rains, be cautious for too much moisture may stimulate soft growth, resulting in decay. Where freezing is a possibility or even a constant problem, do not prune woody plants that are somewhat tender in your area, as bougainvillea, Chinese hibiscus, and eugenia. If frost is predicted, bank these and other plants with soil or place straw or dried leaves around them. Small specimens can be covered with baskets or cartons.

Tree and shrub planting can be continued all winter in the warmest regions, some possibilities including Chinese hibiscus, jasmines, lantanas,

*Palms and banana in New Orleans patio garden. Where cool in winter, as here, banana is likely to die back to ground, but new growth comes vigorously from roots in the spring.*

*Bougainvillea is perhaps the most dazzling and spectacular vine for the Deep South, whether trained on a fence, wall, or trellis. Where winterkill occurs, prune in early spring.*

loquats, oleanders, poinsettias, and pyracanthas. Think too in terms of winter-flowering kinds—camellias, corylopsis, elaeagnus, laurustinus, sweet olive, winter jasmine, winter honeysuckle, and witch-hazels. Don't forget the birds who eat the fruit-bearing chokeberries, cotoneasters, elaeagnus, hawthorns, privets, pyracanthas, and shrub honeysuckles.

Perennials need attention now. First cut back to the ground stems of those that have finished flowering. Trim tops of bearded iris, destroy dead foliage to prevent borers from spreading, and give them an application of bone meal or superphosphate. Daylilies can be planted, as late fall or early winter setting out will result in strong root development—and better growth in the spring. Old overgrown clumps should be lifted, divided, and replanted. Emphasize chrysanthemums by setting out flowering plants purchased from nurseries, some in pots and others in containers for terrace and doorway decoration. With plants in the garden feed as buds begin to show color; stake and keep well watered. When finished flowering cut stems back to six inches from the ground. Plants are best lifted and separated in the early spring.

In cooler regions tender bulbs like achimenes, caladiums, cannas, and tuberous begonias, will need lifting and storing for the winter. Yet in the Deep South many kinds, hardy and tender, can be planted in early winter. Hardy include daffodils, hyacinths, and tulips which have been pre-cooled ("deep freeze," as they are known). Nearly every kind of hardy bulb can be planted depending on your area. Check with your county agricultural agent if you are in doubt. The extensive list of other bulbs includes agapanthus, alliums (ornamental onions), amaryllis, calla-lilies in white, yellow, and pink; camassias, clivias, dahlias, Dutch iris, freesias, gladiolus, including miniatures; Guernsey lily, ixias, liriopes, narcissus (tender), ornithogalums, oxalis, sparaxis, tritonias, and watsonias. Add to this anemones and ranunculus, though in some areas, as southern California, delay planting until later.

As for annual seeds to sow, they are even more numerous, kinds depending on your climate. Among them you can choose calendulas,

*Where annuals and perennials, as yellow marguerite, bloom in winter, keep snipping faded flowers to maintain a neat and tidy appearance and stimulate more blossoms to develop.*

*Dimorphotheca or cape marigold is a common low annual that abounds in the gardens of Arizona in winter, ever in bloom. Tolerating poor soil, it is perfect for sunny places.*

pansies, snapdragons, and stock, all of which enjoy cool growing conditions. Others are ageratum, annual candytuft, annual carnation, annual phlox, arctotis, California poppies, calliopsis, Chinese forget-me-nots, cosmos, English daisies, larkspur, nasturtiums, petunias, sweet alyssum, and verbenas. One of the best is the annual climber sweet peas. Seed that can be sown in fall should be planted in a trench and in cooler parts of the South covered with a three-inch-thick mulch after the ground freezes. In the northern portions plants will bloom in spring; in the warmer, during winter. Be sure to keep moist in drier areas, as the Southwest, but avoid wetness.

While at it, plant some vegetable seeds—beets, broccoli, Brussels sprouts, cabbage, carrots, collards, endive, kale, lettuce, onions, radishes, Swiss chard, and turnips. These are for the Deep South, and remember to mulch—and feed—for extra good growth.

*Dichondra "lawn" in a California garden, popular variation of turf, will blacken if walked on when frost-covered.*

*Caladium is a common bulb in gardens of the South, adding vibrant color in summer. Lift and store bulbs for winter.*

In colder regions roses will need protection by hilling with soil, rose collars, baskets, cones, or other usual methods, but to a lesser degree than in the North. Cut back tall shoots, remove dead and weak stems, and trim soft growth, leaving major pruning for early spring. Where it is warmer, roses of all kinds can be set out in the late fall or winter.

Keep busy by getting cold-frames and hotbeds ready to give seeds an early start later when weather permits. Take cuttings from geraniums for new plants that will bloom in spring, even during winter if your climate allows. If bougainvilleas and wisterias do not bloom, you can root prune them, that is, dig a circular trench three to four feet away from the trunk to a depth of one and a half to two feet, cutting roots. Then replace soil, adding a shovelful or two of bone meal or superphosphate, fertilizers that encourage flowering. Water and mulch. Before planting annuals and bulbs for winter color, clean beds thoroughly. Remove all weeds and sprinkle the soil with an insecticide and fungicide.

*All kinds of trees and shrubs, as palms, can be planted in fall in the South, including winter where warmest. Always prepare soil well, and water regularly if weather is dry.*

*In late fall and early winter when you have more time on
your hands, make dried bouquets from garden or purchased
material, as yellow yarrow, celosia, and dainty statice.*

To decorate your home indoors in winter, make dried bouquets and arrangements from natural materials, lovelier than artificial. Many dried flowers have brilliant colors—celosias, cockscombs, gomphrenas, statice, straw-flowers, and yellow yarrow. Many foliages as well as grasses and seed pods are equally attractive, among them cycas, lotus pods, palms, pampas grass, sea-oats, and wood-roses.

Due to the longer growing season the southerner's garden tools do not get much chance to rest. If there are some you will not need, clean, oil, and store in a dry place until ready to use again in the early spring, which comes sooner than in the North.

# 2

## Winter in the South

Mid-December to mid-February is the heart of the winter season in the South. Usually January is the coldest month, as it is throughout the country. Contrary to popular opinion, winters are not always mild even in the Deep South. Though plants are not growing actively, tips can be nipped by frost during exceptionally cold spells. Often plants in northern sections, as the Carolinas, escape injury while those along the Gulf Coast and Florida become damaged because growth is soft.

Nevertheless, gardening continues during the winter, more in the Lower or Deep South that extends from California along the Gulf Coast to Florida. At the same time there are protective measures that can be taken to guard plants against partial or permanent injury.

Bulbs need winter attention. Dahlias in warmer parts will flower in winter but should be lifted around the middle of February. Wash soil from tubers, cut off diseased portions, place in boxes or other containers, and cover with peat moss or other medium, keeping moist but not wet. When new shoots appear and are about two or three inches high, divide clumps so each piece has at least one visible eye from which growth will appear. Replant outdoors in soil well supplied with peat moss, leafmold, compost, or other organic matter.

Bulbs in winter storage, like caladiums which need to be kept at 70° to 75° F., should be checked periodically because they will rot if stored where too cold. If too moist or wet, place them outdoors in the sun for a day or two to dry out. If any show signs of shriveling, sprinkle with water.

Many kinds of tender bulbs can be planted in January in the warmest areas, including alstromerias, amaryllis, anemones, freesias, ginger-lilies, gladiolus, hedychium, liriopes, oxalis, and ranunculus. From the middle toward the end of February others can be set out, but this depends on the area. Some to try are acidantheras, agapanthus, calla-lilies, crinums, Dutch, English, and Spanish iris, montbretias, tigridias, tuberoses, watsonias, and zephyranthes. Precooled Dutch bulbs, as daffodils, hyacinths,

*In the Lower South amaryllis bulbs can be planted in open ground in winter, but need lifting where cooler. They need sun and well-drained soil to perform well.*

and tulips should be set out as soon as available in your area.

Tender bulbs are easily handled and protected. More difficult to survive freezing spells are the tropical plants, which can tolerate little or no frost. No part of the Continental United States is tropical. Florida is actually subtropical, yet many tropical plants like allamandas, bananas, copperleafs, crotons, and pentas can be grown. If acclimatized to cold gradually, injury is apt to be slight. One method for handling tropicals, if the plants are small enough, is to lift, pot, and take them indoors where frosts are expected.

*Lift calla-lily bulbs after cold or frost has browned leaves, and store in dry peat, sand, or other medium.*

Some form of winter protection should be given tender plants that cannot be brought indoors. If a cold snap is predicted, many plants can be covered with boxes, baskets, or cartons at the end of the day. Do not use metal as it conducts cold. The bases of tender plants can be banked with soil that is removed after the freeze. Take the soil away in the early morning before the sun shines on the plants. Then water and spray well with the hose or sprinkler.

Plants can be protected by coverings, as wrapping with burlap attached to stakes. Be certain to place the burlap, cloth, or other material around and over the stakes without touching the leaves, which may "burn" if there is contact. Also protect the bases of plants with a collar of peat moss, leafmold, straw, pine needles, wood chips, leaves, Spanish moss, or other material. Burlap will protect a plant if the temperature drops briefly to 28° F. More effective is wrapping entire plants with old blankets or double layers of sheets before sundown, removing them early the next morning.

Smudge pots will raise the temperature six degrees, and orchard heaters, fires, and fans—often used in citrus groves—will make the air ten degrees warmer. Freezing will be prevented if these devices are allowed to burn until the early morning hours or when it is safe to shut them off.

One of the best and most widely practiced methods of protecting plants is to keep them well watered. Specimens well supplied with moisture stand a better chance of surviving than those that are dry. Keep plants of questionable hardiness moist at all times, but water particularly if a cold snap is expected. Do not water tops of plants; rather soak or irrigate soil in the late afternoon or evening.

If trees, shrubs, and other plants are covered with frost in the early morning, much damage can be prevented if they are washed immediately with the hose or with sprinklers. Avoid walking on lawns covered by frost, particularly dichondra, as every footstep will cause the "turf" to turn black. If tender plants have been blackened by frost, whether protected or not, do not prune immediately—except for poinsettias—as other freezes might follow. Pruning only exposes them to additional injury, so leave them untouched until the middle or the latter part of March when new growth will show the amount of winterkilling. Although many plants will develop new sprouts after they have been damaged by frosts, it is sound practice to wait until vigorous growth starts before pruning. Early pruning tends to stimulate premature growth, which is likely to be killed by unexpected cold weather.

Other steps can be taken to keep difficult-to-grow plants in good condition. Avoid early feeding and cultivating, which is bound to promote soft growth. Refrain from customary pruning in late fall as, again, new growth may be forced when dormancy is the goal. Another worthwhile practice is to wrap trunks and stems of not-too-tender trees and shrubs with newspapers and bank them with soil around the base.

Two popular shrubs grown all over the South—azaleas and camellias —should not be fed until after flowering. And this means in *spring*. Use products that are acid in content. If they become infested with scale, a common pest, spray with an oil emulsion following directions for amounts. Do the same with gardenias, which are also inclined to pick up this stubborn problem.

Chinese hibiscus where not reliably top hardy can be mulched around the base, while bananas can be wrapped with cloth, burlap, or paper to prevent freezing. Even if bananas die back to the ground (a frequent occurrence), the plants have an amazing capacity for revival, and will send forth strong, sturdy stems from the roots with warmer weather. Prepare the vegetable garden to have it ready for March planting.

Many perennials start growing in January in the southernmost parts. When young shoots grow two to four inches, lift and divide them. Enrich soil with organic material and sprinkle lightly with mixed fertilizer. These perennials include chrysanthemums, daylilies, fall asters, physostegias, phlox, and shasta daisies. Where they are hardy, along the south-

*Gladiolus bulbs can be lifted when leaves have turned yellow or brown without frost. Cut tops, then store.*

*Either before storing or planting, remove dead bulb, the original, at the base. Plant new ones on the top.*

ern border of the country, overcrowded cannas can be dug, separated, and reset.

Roses should come in for their share of attention. Established bushes can be transplanted in midwinter when they are dormant. Feed in warmer regions in late January, but in most areas the two weeks in February are considered better, usually when leaf buds begin to swell. A root feeder, a tool inserted two or more feet into the ground, is excellent for roses—and other woody plants—because nutrients are distributed close to the roots. Similar care applies to climbing roses. When pruning, cut back to obviously healthy wood, eliminating any that has been frozen.

Lawns can be repaired by seeding or sodding, while old ones can be redone. New lawns that were started several weeks previously and have been mowed three or four times can be fed with a mixed fertilizer, high in nitrogen, if weather is warm.

Do not forget to prune fruit trees, cutting tops of figs and other kinds, removing suckers at the bases. Deciduous fruit trees can be pruned in midwinter and then given a dormant spray. Leave major pruning until danger of cold is past. In the Lower South all kinds of fruit trees can be planted in January, but farther north wait until February. Be sure to stake, using soft cord that will not cut the bark.

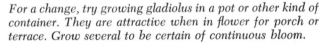

*For a change, try growing gladiolus in a pot or other kind of container. They are attractive when in flower for porch or terrace. Grow several to be certain of continuous bloom.*

Both January and February are excellent planting months for reliably hardy trees, shrubs, and other plants starting in the southernmost areas and proceeding north according to the weather. All varieties of balled and burlapped evergreens can be set out, as well as plants in containers. Slit the cans with tin shears, but if unable to do it yourself, your nurseryman can be of help. Bare-rooted stock can be planted in January in the warmest regions, including such kinds as almonds, Chinese magnolia, crab apples, crape-myrtles, flowering peaches and plums, and roses. Farther north, February is the better month for planting. Use organic matter, such as peat moss or compost, in the soil with bare-rooted stock. Feed only on the surface after growth has started and you can see that plants have become established.

Tropical plants should not be planted until the end of March, when danger of frost is over. They will then have a long growing season with sufficient time to become well established and will be better able to withstand the cold. The winter season is an excellent time to plant azaleas and camellias.

Annuals flower all winter in the South. In the warmest regions ageratum, bachelor's-buttons, calendulas, calliopsis, clarkias, cleomes, larkspur, pinks, poppies, and snapdragons can be sown. In February, plant seed of godetias and schizanthus indoors for an early start. When set outdoors, flowering will be completed before hot weather appears.

Small plants of annuals that are tender can be protected against cold snaps with Spanish moss or several thicknesses of newspapers around the base, held in place with stones. Banking with earth is another practical technique.

Feed annuals to keep flowering, including calendulas, Iceland poppies, larkspur, pansies, snapdragons, stock, and sweet peas. Keep removing the faded blossoms to improve appearance and encourage more bloom. Plants can be fed every two or three weeks with liquid fertilizer, as 6-8-8, until late in spring, when they will have spent themselves.

As for pruning, go light on broad-leaved evergreens and shrubs which flower early in the spring. Such kinds are exochordas, spireas, and viburnums should be pruned after flowering. December and January are the dry months in Florida so water regularly, soaking the soil to a depth of several inches. A thorough watering once a week is enough. It is best done in the morning, as watering late in the day encourages fungus diseases.

Finally, do not forget the birds in the gardens of the South. Though winters are comparatively mild in contrast to the North, birds often have difficulty getting food during cold periods. Suet, bread crumbs, and wild and other seed mixtures will bring many attractive species for you to enjoy.

# 3

## Early Spring in the South

SPRING IS a fleeting season in the South, its length depending on the temperatures in the different areas. Since it arrives throughout most of the South by April, gardening should be planned to coincide with the developing warm weather.

In some years a late freeze presents problems. An unseasonable frost can cause extensive damage to young tender foliage and flower buds. Under these conditions hasten to cover plants with baskets, boxes, cloth, or burlap. If plants have been touched by frost, a thorough sprinkling of the leaves with the hose or sprinkler system should be given in the early morning before the sun rises, as this will prevent injury. In the event of a cold spell do not remove all leaves from perennials that start growth early. Loosen the leaves and be prepared to replace if frost danger threatens.

When the weather stays uniformly warm cut back tops of such perennials as chrysanthemums, which can be lifted and separated. Retain the more vigorous outer shoots. Also take cuttings of favorite varieties to make new plants. Root them in a 50-50 mixture of peat moss and sand. Other perennials, including fall asters, shasta daisies, and daylilies, are best divided early.

Cleanup also means cultivating the soil by adding organic matter to improve its texture and friability. Soak any plants that appear to be dry, but avoid wetting foliage because moisture promotes mildew. Then apply a mulch, fine-textured for flower beds, coarse for tree and shrub plantings. Often soot and grime gather on evergreens during winter, especially in gardens in large industrial cities. Wash them down vigorously with the hose so the stomata (porelike openings in the leaves) can breathe freely. A greening lawn indicates the need for spring feeding. Use a prepared all-purpose kind that includes weed killers.

Now is the time to set out all kinds of trees, shrubs, vines, roses, perennials, annuals, and bulbs—hardy and tender. These include, among

*Outdoor work area gets no rest where gardening continues all winter. Keep as neat as possible to make easier to use.*

*Gardenia is a cherished shrub in many southern gardens. Spray with malathion if plagued with mealy bugs.*

*Where frost threatens, container plants—as this palm and Chinese hibiscus—can easily be taken indoors for the night.*

woody kinds, azaleas, bougainvilleas, camellias, crape-myrtles, Chinese hibiscus, oleanders, and plumbago, a popular shrub with pale blue flowers. What and when you plant depends on the part of the South in which you garden. Hardiness is the prime factor to consider. With tropicals wait until late March when just about all chance of frost has passed. You can make new plants to increase your stock with cuttings or by air layering.

Pruning at this time is equally important. Begin when new buds are starting to swell. It is best to wait as long as possible, then cut back to live wood and shape as desired. With shrub roses prune back to live, healthy stems. Do the same with climbers, hybrid teas, floribundas, and other roses, newly planted or established. Apply a balanced fertilizer; dig it in lightly and water thoroughly. Then embark on a regular weekly spray program to keep plants healthy.

*Charming veranda with container plants in an Arizona garden in winter. For new effects, move them around.*

*For best flowering, hardy chrysanthemums should be lifted and separated in the spring. Prepare soil and label varieties.*

Prune spring-flowering woody plants sparingly, but with summer-flowering kinds you can be more severe. Remove branches damaged by frost on oleanders; pruning can be hard since flower clusters are borne on the new growth. Do the same with altheas (rose of sharon), vitexes, and crape-myrtles, which flower from midsummer into fall.

Tender bulbs, whether lifted in the fall or winter or left in the ground, can be set out—spectacular crinums, dahlias, gladiolus, tuberoses, and watsonias. All provide color for a long period. For continuous display annuals fill the bill. Set them out to your heart's desire—balsams, globe amaranths, marigolds, morning-glories, portulacas, snapdragons, zinnias, and others.

Keep blooming annuals neat and vigorous by removing faded flowers. Diseased plants should be sprayed with an insecticide-fungicide, a recommended practice to destroy eggs of hibernating insects and to check fungi that may appear later when the weather becomes hot and humid. When setting out young plants, prepare beds by digging in organic matter and a mixed fertilizer such as 5-10-5. For early bloom from annuals, start seed indoors in flats or other containers and transplant later to the garden when weather settles. Then yours will be a garden of dazzling colors, a pleasure from the time the first blooms appear until wintertime.

*Seeds of morning-glories, as this popular Heavenly Blue, can be sown as soon as frost-free weather comes. Give good drainage.*

# INDEX

*Entries in italics refer to photographs*

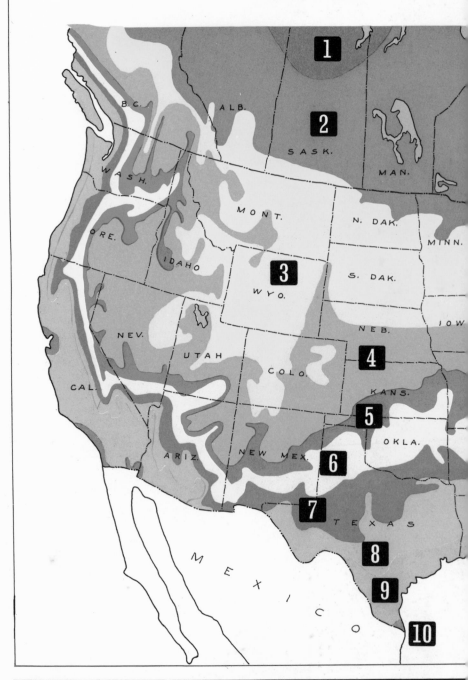

# HARDIN
## UNITED STAT